THRIVERS

AN ENTREPRENEUR'S FABLE

VANCE BROWN

JOHN BOLIN

Edited by
JOHN BLASE

WE HAPPY FEW PUBLISHING

ISBN 9781983377204

Second Edition

 Created with Vellum

CONTENTS

INTRODUCTION

A note to the reader

You have in your hands a fable, which by definition is "a short story conveying a moral." The moral, or lesson, is one that I have learned and continue to learn, and it has made all the difference in how I approach my business and relationships with family and friends. The best lessons typically are learned through struggles, failures, and disappointments—and that is indeed the case for me.

Some entrepreneurs' highest priority is making money (whether or not they choose to admit it), while others most value a life of meaning. The reality is that most of us want both. Unfortunately, we all lean with a mindset and skill set that favors one over the other, just like most people are either more left-brained (analytical) or right-brained (artistic). The same is typically true of entrepreneurship. Rarely are entrepreneurs good at both, yet I believe you can have both with the right training and self-awareness.

I've now learned there is a way to swing your sword and

live from the heart at the same time. This is not an either/or paradigm but a non-dualistic way to build a successful business and have a life of meaning. Those who can do both are "Thrivers." The obvious question is, "How does one become a Thriver with the ability to change the world?" That is the lesson we all want to learn. Thanks for joining me on this journey.

—Vance Brown

1

YESTERDAY

It seems like only yesterday. I was a bright-eyed college grad, determined to take life by the horns, change the world, and make a million by thirty.

But here I am, forty-five years old with high blood pressure, less hair, and more unpaid bills. Surely my best life is behind me. To top it off, my glasses are fogged, and my hair is dripping wet because I didn't count on the rain.

Yeah, I know. I hate all those negative thoughts, too. I have them all the time. What happened to that young, passionate visionary and dreamer, the man I used to be? Come on, Chad! Snap out of it.

I close my eyes and shake my head. *Refocus. Breathe.* This deal could change everything. I know that. This is easily the most important meeting of my career. The truth is I'm still that passionate visionary. I know that too. But what I've never been able to do well is execute. So while my business has been exciting, it's also felt like running a race in only one shoe.

But maybe today will be different. Maybe today's my day —when everything will fall in line, come together. Maybe today I get the other shoe.

I run my fingers through my hair, trying to get as much water out as I can. It's no use. A bell chimes, and I step into the empty elevator. As the door closes behind me, I begin to rehearse my pitch.

The elevator door opens to the forty-second floor. This is the moment I've been waiting for. I step out into a minimalist reception area. A granite sign commands the wall: Invest-Corp. An attractive young woman sits behind a desk, probably in her late twenties or early thirties. She wears hipster glasses and has black hair bleached at the tips.

"Mr. Banning?"

"Yes. That's me."

"They're ready for you in the conference room. Here, follow me," she says and leads me down a hallway. "You look like you could use a towel."

"Yeah, the rain, it caught me by surprise."

She laughs, then turns and walks backward for a moment. "I'm Cameron. Good to meet you, Mr. Banning."

"I'm Chad. Nice to meet you too."

Cameron stops in front of a set of double doors. "Don't worry. You'll do great."

"Thanks." I turn, open the door, and step inside.

The boardroom is impressive and impersonal. Two of the walls are ceiling-to-floor glass, and the other two are stark white with some sort of black wire, three-dimensional sculptures protruding from them. The conference table is made of thick glass, surrounded by at least a dozen Scandinavian-looking swivel chairs. Sitting in the chairs are half a dozen people staring back at me.

For a moment I want to run. I'm not good with this type of audience. I'm a salesman, not a negotiator. I thought about bringing my business partner, Eric, but I'm the CEO and it's good for me to do this. At least that's what I keep telling myself. After all, I am the one who started the company. I should be the one to take it to the next level.

A big man wearing a Hawaiian shirt stands and extends his hand to me.

"You must be Chad," he says. "Looks like you didn't plan on the rain."

The others all laugh, and I relax a bit and make the rounds, shaking hands and swapping smiles. The Hawaiian shirt is named Marcus. He's the managing partner of Invest-Corp and, from what I've heard, a take-no-prisoners negotiator. The two suits at the table are lawyers. A young guy sporting a beard and a T-shirt is VP of engineering. And a tall, thin woman in her fifties is the CFO. After the introductions, everyone takes a seat.

FOR THE NEXT THIRTY MINUTES, I stand at the end of the table and give the sales pitch of my life. And it's good. I'm in my element. I use my knack for storytelling and some cool slides and videos to sell the value and opportunity of my company, Sensors Everywhere. I even have numbers and statistics and testimonials to back up everything.

I tell them how I got the idea for the company after a trip to Home Depot, shopping for a sprinkler head, when I saw a display for a home security and climate control system. The system is basically a series of sensors that helps regulate temperatures, monitors hallways and entryways, and sends information to your smartphone.

I tell them I realized that if there were sensors for temperature and home security, there could be sensors for a lot of other things. Turns out, I was right. There were sensors being built for everything from kitchen appliances to cars and even sprinklers. That's when I figured that if the sensor business was exploding, someone needed to be building and programming all those sensors. *Voila!*—Sensors Everywhere, a platform and API hub for all things involving electronic sensors. We know we can be a major force with the Internet of Things.

Everyone is engaged, even the suits. I believe I have them in the palm of my hand.

"So that's when I hired Eric."

"Who's Eric?" the CFO lady asks.

"Well, he's my partner. I hired him as soon as I realized I needed someone who was more detailed than me. Eric heads up our systems development and the operations aspects of the company."

What I don't tell them is that Eric can drive me nuts. He's the opposite of me in almost every way. I'm an optimist and he's a pessimist, or as he calls it, *a realist.* I love to dream about new ideas and corporate culture improvements. He's mostly interested in process and the bottom line, which doesn't include a lot of my creative ideas.

But at the time, I was desperate for someone to help me run the business, and I needed someone who was organized and focused. I needed an architect of growth, someone who knew the nuts and bolts of running an actual, sustainable, high-growth business. That was Eric. When I hired him, he was coming out of a pretty nasty divorce that had cost him a lot of his net worth. I was able to scoop him up for a lot less than he was used to making.

I tell these venture capitalists about Eric and the other executive team members and give a thorough review of our entire organization. They ask lots of questions. I try to give good answers to everything. I paint a clear picture of our history and then a vivid vision of what the future of Sensors

Everywhere could be, with a little help from our friends with some cash. My pitch is like a religious experience. The table is willing converts.

I close my laptop, step back, and twist open a bottle of mineral water as if opening a cold IPA at the end of the day.

Marcus grins. "Chad, I think you could persuade God to follow you. We don't need to spend any time on this. We've looked over your financials, heard your proposal, and now we're ready to offer you a deal. All we need is your name on the line on this term sheet, and we'll draft the definitive agreements." He passes a sheet of paper across the table to me and points to the dollar amount of their offer—$5 million.

Don't lose it, Chad. Breathe, man. Breathe.

As I scan the key terms, it's quickly evident the overall deal is painfully one-sided. I would become a minority share-holder while InvestCorp would own the majority. I would lose control of the company. Marcus would essentially be my boss.

I swallow hard and speak. "It looks like you're proposing a pretty hefty percentage for your side of the table."

Marcus grins again; he's been in this scenario before. "Yeah, well, we're the ones taking the big risk here. Truth is, your company lives in the red and burns through cash. We're very impressed with all you've done to get the company to where it is today, but your company is not sustainable. There's no future for you without a pretty big infusion of capital, from our side of the table."

I'm not nearly as confident I can do this on my own. Now I'm wishing Eric were here.

My blood pressure is rising. I'm certain my face shows it. What I wouldn't give right now for Harry Potter's cloak of invisibility. It's funny, that image coming to mind. My son Adam and I read through all the Potter books together, watched all the movies. The cloak of invisibility would give me what I need—just a few unexposed minutes to think.

"Chad, you're really not in a position to negotiate here. You're outta time. You need a miracle, and we're it."

My initial impression of Marcus is fading fast. His boast and swagger are making me want to throttle him, not partner with him. But I'm paralyzed, like a dog in a muzzle.

"Tell you what, Chad. Take a couple of weeks to think it over. We've got until October 1 to make this deal happen. We'll look to hear from you then. In the meantime, we'll draft the definitive documents to get this deal closed. Fair enough, champ?"

Champ? Really? Can this get any more condescending?

"Oh, there's one last contingency to make this deal happen, chief."

Now it's chief?

"I'm sorry," I say. "Contingency?"

The CFO speaks. "While we're very impressed with where you've managed to take the company, Chad, we believe that for Sensors Everywhere to thrive in terms of growth and sustainability, we need a new CEO."

And it just got more condescending. I blink. I cannot believe what I'm hearing.

"It's not that we want you out, Chad. We just want you to be you, and you're the salesman, the evangelist preaching to the biggest clients and analysts. While you're doing that, someone else without your emotional attachments to the company and the people can lead it to the next level. You have taken this company further than most founders are able. But there are some important organizational changes that need to happen, and we just don't think you have the natural capacity to do what is necessary."

"Chad, do you know what your *real* problem is?"

Wow! That is quite the question. Now he really has my attention, although I'm not sure I am ready to hear what he has to say.

"No, Marcus, what is my *real* problem?" At this point, I'm not even trying to hide the irritation and sarcasm.

Looking me straight in the eyes, Marcus proclaims, "No offense, Chad, but you are too much of a *missionary*."

Now my blood pressure is boiling over. Damn straight I am offended! Should I give him a sucker punch right between the eyes? And should I tell him what I am thinking? *Marcus, your problem is that you are too much of a f***ing mercenary*. I don't say it. Instead, I sit there paralyzed. Heck, I even feel bad having such thoughts, given my religious upbringing. Just being real. But the truth is that I'm just such a wimp!

The CFO speaks again. "Don't worry. You'll still own more shares of the company than any other individual. You'll still have a lot of influence. And with a seasoned CEO in the chair, we all win. One day you'll have more money than you can spend, and your children's lives will be taken care of." She looks around the room, and everyone grins.

Forget the cloak of invisibility, I need a magician's broomstick to get out of this room and fast. But this is not fiction. Dear God, this is really happening. Marcus puts his hand on my shoulder and leads me out into the hallway. His hand is deathly cold. Maybe it's just me. "Remember, Chad, we're your miracle. Cameron will validate your parking." He squeezes my shoulder, winks, and steps back into the boardroom.

I'm afraid I may vomit.

When I get to the lobby, I reach for my phone to call Eric. I explain everything and tell him we have a deadline for our decision. He doesn't say anything at first.

Then, "Well, I guess we should at least think about it. We don't have many options."

I want to scream and say, *"What? You can't be serious. Oh, you are serious, aren't you? You just want to cash out and move on. You don't care about me or Sensors Everywhere or any of this, just what's good for Eric, huh?"*

But I don't say any of that. All I can manage is an exhausted "Okay." That seems like all I can ever manage these days. And I hate it.

THE LYFT DRIVER is waiting by the curb in an older model Volvo station wagon, windows down. A college-age kid sits behind the wheel. The app said his name was Ryan.

He leans his head out. "Chad?"

"That's me. Ryan?"

He nods, and I jump in.

I'm in no mood to chat, but I get the sense that Ryan isn't picking up on it. He verifies our destination, begins to accelerate, and then turns his head.

"Well, happy Friday. You got plans for the weekend?"

I still feel like I could be sick, and I've got to try to engage with my wife, Maggie, and my three kids tonight. Not to mention pack for a weekend trip. I'm not really in the mood for small talk. I take a deep breath.

"Uh, yeah, actually. I'm headed to Colorado."

"Colorado? That's cool. A little vaca?"

"I wish. No, I leave tomorrow for an entrepreneur's retreat.'"

Ryan nods in approval. "Sounds cool."

At least that's the way my wife billed it. She set it all up and presented it to me on my birthday. It's an incredibly kind gift, just like

Maggie, but leaving town after everything that has happened today feels foolish.

"So, what's it all about?" Ryan asks. "I'm working on my business degree. Sounds like the kind of thing I'd be into."

"Well, a reclusive venture capitalist and business turn-around expert named Mark Rollins bought a ranch high in the Colorado Rockies and started running retreats for entrepreneurial business leaders."

"Wow. So it's sort of a big deal."

"I suppose," I say. "Only a limited number of spaces are available. The learning sessions 'push you to your edge'—at least that's what they say. Oh, and all the food is world-class." I smile for the first time since the meeting.

Maybe that's exactly what I need right now. It's just the "right now" part that's throwing me.

Before I know it, we pull up to my house and I jump out. Maggie's there as I open the front door.

"Well, how'd it go?" she asks.

From my eyes and my dramatic sigh, she reads the moment like a book. "So, not great, huh?"

"It was okay, Maggie, just okay. We got an offer, but it feels like a deal with the devil. They want more than half the company. And they want to find a new CEO."

Just then, my youngest, Lizzy, comes bounding to the front door.

"Daddy!" she says as she jumps up and swings on my arm. I smile and lift her into the air. Even though my day was tough, seeing Lizzy always reminds me of what matters most. Still, my mind is preoccupied.

Maggie's smart. We've been married twenty years, so she knows this has stunned me. She simply steps forward and kisses me. "Sounds like you need the Entrepreneur's Retreat." She says it with a coy smile. She's proud of herself. "C'mon, dinner's almost ready, and the kids are all home at the same time. A miracle, right?"

The kitchen island reveals dinner—pizza from our favorite local joint. Maggie winks at me. Adam, my seventeen-year-old, and his fifteen-year-old brother, Will, break away from whatever video game they're playing in the basement to join us. We grab slices and drinks and sit around the kitchen table.

Everybody seems in a great mood, except me. But it's funny, even with the crappy day I've had, I'm extremely thankful for the family surrounding me. I'd die for these people, no questions asked. I want my children to fly further than I have, but I also want them to discover and then hang on tightly to who they truly are. Maggie and I usually see things differently, but on this we agree.

I believe that, but then I turn around and contradict myself in conversations with our kids. This plays out in our dinner discussion.

Adam got accepted to USC, but he wants to go somewhere small and get an art degree. A part of me loves the art idea, his passion around it, and he's truly gifted. But this comes out of my mouth over pizza: "Why not go to USC—it is USC, after all—and get a business degree, something so you can support yourself financially while you pursue your art on the side?"

"That's what you did, Dad, and I don't want to do that," he says. Then, being the smart kid he is, he adds, "And what about living from my true and authentic self?" His younger siblings look at each other, then me, then Maggie. Everybody at the table knows I'm busted, most of all me.

"I want to make a difference, Dad. I believe I can best do that with my art. And I don't want to wait until I'm your age to start."

That last bit stings. In a sense, I know he's right. He might also see things a little differently if he'd been with me today in that boardroom full of sharks. Making money is not everything, but it sure comes in handy in the real world. How else could we afford · this house, our groceries, their college education?

Maggie saves dinner by grabbing the tiramisu from the fridge. "I thought a little dessert would be a nice way to send you off for a few days." It was.

2

UP AND AWAY

The next morning, I'm still thinking about yesterday. I feel discouraged and beaten. I see Eric in the driveway. He offered to take me to the airport. As I grab my bags and step out of the door, I hear Maggie's angry voice. "Are you seriously leaving without even saying goodbye?"

I turn around.

"Chad, you've been distant a lot lately," she starts. "You're physically here, but your mind is a thousand miles away. I need you to be present. The kids need you to be present. I hope you can go on this retreat and get some perspective. If something doesn't change, you could lose a whole lot more than your company."

"Wow, that feels harsh! What is that supposed to mean?" I respond. "That's a lot to carry as I leave for a couple of days."

"Seriously? Come on, Chad!" she adds. "This is not a new discussion. This has been a core issue in our marriage. Don't act surprised, and please don't pull the victim card!"

"Okay." My tone no doubt reveals the futility I feel. "We'll talk more when I get back."

Eric is waiting in his car. I had agreed to his offer of taking me to the airport in hopes we could talk before I was on some mountain peak, beyond cell range. It's about ten minutes down the road before he says anything.

"I believe we should take the deal, Chad."

I pause a beat. "Seriously?"

"Yes, I do. Look, it's not an ideal offer—bailouts never are—and I hate that they're asking you to step down as CEO, I really do. But it could be the best thing for the company. InvestCorp's reputation for business turnaround and acceleration is solid. They do this all the time."

"So we should all just happily dilute our shares while I smile and step away from something I built from nothing and entrust it all to these, these mercenaries?" I say as I look at him, incredulous.

Eric is silent for a few minutes, and then he takes the exit ramp marked DEPARTURES.

"Yes, Chad, that's exactly what I think."

I'M in the security line, basically undressing so as to hopefully avoid a pat-down or feel-up. I make it through the scanner successfully and then begin redressing.

What a perfect metaphor for my life right now. Over the last few years I've felt like I've been undressed, stripped of those things that matter to me. My love for my work has faded. The pressure I have felt for the past couple of years has been intense. I've not felt like much of a husband to Maggie or a father to the kids. And here I stand, having been incredibly vulnerable to the TSA's scanner just like I was in InvestCorp's boardroom, and I fear both have seen that I have no backbone and a shrinking heart.

I'm not sure how the guy who is traveling to the "by-invitation-only" Entrepreneur's Retreat gets to board with Group 5, but yet another on-target metaphor of my current life. But a little redemption comes in the form of 18A, a window seat, my preference. I sit, settle in, buckle up, and find myself immediately lulled by what's on the other side of three panes of plexiglass—nothing. I pray no one occupies 18B.

So much for prayer. She steps from the aisle into the row, dressed to the nines with a designer bag in one hand and a dog carrier in the other. I'd guess she's about sixty. She slings the bag up top, but the dog stays down with us.

"Don't worry, honey. Jem'll behave," she reassures. Jem, I assume, is the dog. This should be fun.

My phone buzzes, a text message from Marcus. My gut tightens.

Chad, no need to respond. Just know we're ready to pull the trigger. Documents are nearly done. Trust me, this will be good for everybody. Talk soon.

I start to text back when 18B interrupts: "Be a dear and keep an eye on Jem?" She winks and is gone before I can respond. Between the text from Marcus and my new Jem duty, I don't realize an older gentleman has stopped at our row.

"18C," he says to himself, then looks at me and Jem.

"I've been assured he'll behave," I say. He smiles warmly and starts to take his seat when 18B returns.

"Well, aren't I the lucky duck in the middle of you two dears. Pardon me while I squeeze back in before you buckle up."

"Certainly," he says. "I'm Jack." He extends his hand to her.

"I am Elizabeth. This is Jem. And that's, well, I didn't get your name, sugar."

"Chad," I say. "Good to meet you all."

As the pilot carries us to cruising altitude, Jack and Elizabeth are deep in conversation. Jem is behaving, as promised. I unwind my headphones, lean against the three panes of plexiglass, and drift off to a playlist Adam created for me. The last thing I remember is a line from The Beatles: "*Suddenly, I'm not half the man I used to be.*"

Perfect.

3

INTO THE WILD

Since the retreat is in the Rocky Mountains, I figure I'll play along. I'm given a choice of cars at the rental desk, and I pick a Jeep. To further seal the deal, I play John Denver's "Rocky Mountain High" as I wind my way up a narrow canyon dirt road with the top down and the volume up. I glance at my phone—*no cell service*. It's strange; I feel alone but also somehow lighter.

I don't consider myself much of an outdoorsman, but wanderlust has always been a part of who I am. It was stirred again several years ago when I read Jon Krakauer's *Into the Wild*. As I boarded a flight to London, I discovered someone had left their copy in the seat-back pocket in front of me. It felt serendipitous, especially since the owner had written his first name inside: *Chad*. Mere coincidence? I don't know, but it gave me a little hope at the time.

I was quickly swept up in the story of Chris McCandless, the twenty-four-year-old honors graduate, star athlete, and beloved brother and son from a wealthy but dysfunctional

East Coast family. With a head full of Jack London and Henry David Thoreau, McCandless renamed himself "Alexander Supertramp," cut all family ties, gave his trust fund to charity, and set off on a two-year journey that led him to Alaska.

As I continue up the mountain, words from the book that I underlined and later copied and taped above my desk rush back to my mind: "Nothing is more damaging to the adventurous spirit within a man than a secure future. The very basic core of a man's living spirit is his passion for adventure. The joy of life comes from our encounters with new experiences, and hence there is no greater joy than to have an endlessly changing horizon, for each day to have a new and different sun."

Along with towering trees on one side of the road and very narrow drop-offs with no guardrails on the other, these words excite me. They also scare me.

I slow the Jeep and pull up to an entryway made of giant timbers. Hanging from the top is a rustic sign: *Six Peaks Ranch*. The road beneath the sign is covered with golden aspen leaves, like it might lead to Oz. As I drive under the sign, I am immediately surrounded by several guys in their twenties. They look like something from a Silicon Valley ad, all shadow beards and designer glasses.

Twentysomething guy #1 approaches the driver's side: "Welcome to the Entrepreneur's Retreat! You must be Chad."

"Yeah, that's right. How'd you know?"

"Just a wild guess," he says with a sly smile. "That and I'm pretty good matching pictures to faces." He reveals his clipboard, complete with my LinkedIn profile and picture. "I'm Dylan, one of the staff around here for the weekend. We're honored to have a successful entrepreneur with such a great story with us. We're excited you've chosen to share your time with us."

I confess to being caught just a little off guard. "Uh, thanks, Dylan. So where do I go from here?"

"Just follow the signs to the main lodge; it's called Wild Rose Lodge. There you'll receive your room assignment. Plus, you can mingle with the others during a special welcome reception. We'll have our first session there tonight."

Dylan taps the hood of the Jeep, steps back, and extends his arm in the direction of the lodge. In contrast to the meetings I've been in lately where there was so much subtext to every conversation, my exchange with Dylan feels life-giving, like he actually cares.

The interior of Wild Rose Lodge looks rustic but nice. I step up to a registration table where a woman hands me a packet and name badge.

"Looks like you're in the Sugarloaf cabin," she says.

"Is that a good thing?" I ask.

"Yes, that's Jack's favorite cabin."

"Jack?"

"Jack Angel. He's the table host and main facilitator for your group this weekend."

I recognize his name from the information about the retreat I'd received earlier, but I don't know much more than that.

"Jack is a bit of an enigma," she says. "Most people don't know that he's been one of the most successful software entrepreneurs of the past decade. He's done it quietly and under the radar. And now he loves to find leaders and organizations with a compelling story and a passion to turn it into a reality."

This woman is becoming more and more animated.

"Trust me, you're one of the lucky ones to have him as your group leader. Stick around and see."

I turn to walk away, but I hear her voice trailing after me. "And whatever you do, don't miss the opening session. Mark Rollins will be presenting our North Star."

"The North Star?" I ask, turning back toward her.

"It's the framework for everything we do. We navigate all the other big ideas around here by the North Star. Miss that and you might as well go home." She smiles, not like she's flirting but like she cares. *Authentic*, that's the word.

AFTER UNPACKING my things and taking a brief power nap, I'm back at Wild Rose Lodge. The room that earlier felt like a hotel check-in now has a killer event vibe—still rustic while appropriately upscale. Low lights. Open bar. The movie soundtrack music gives a dramatic sense to the room.

I spot a table that has my name on it. I naturally check out the other names to see whom I'll be sitting with tonight—

Kyle Jenson, CEO of a company called Splash, Inc.

Alex Miller, from the Barbarian Group, whatever that is.

Maya Fontaine, independent artist, no company listed.

Evan Stack, co-founder of Big Boss Games.

Jack Angel, facilitator.

And . . . me. Seems like a pretty diverse group.

"Hi, Chad." A big guy with a wide smile is standing in front of me, eyeing my name tag. I look at his and see his name and "Splash, Inc."

"You're Kyle?"

"Yep, that's me," he says quietly.

"It's good to meet you." We shake hands, although his is more like a paw.

"Good to meet you too," Kyle says. "Is this your first Entrepreneur's Retreat here at Six Peaks?" I get the sense that this isn't exactly Kyle's comfort zone.

"Yes," I say. "How about you?"

"It is." He leans in toward me. "Did you know one thousand people applied to be here this weekend?"

"You're kidding." I had no idea it was so exclusive.

"Not kidding. And only sixty of us were chosen. Sort of makes you feel awesome about yourself, right?" He grins.

I'm not sure if the facts Kyle laid out made me feel good or if it was just Kyle himself. Whatever it was, it worked. I can't help but grin in return. "So, what does Splash do?" I ask.

A young guy who'd been standing nearby suddenly edges into our conversation, extending his hand toward us. He looks to be twenty, barely, and is sporting a beard, jeans, and a T-shirt.

"Don't tell us. I did my homework," the young entrepreneur says. "You guys dig wells and do clean water work overseas, right?"

"Basically, yes. That's what we do," Kyle says as we all shake hands.

"But you're not the only one who did his homework," Kyle adds awkwardly. "Let's see. Evan Stack"—pausing, as if he's running through a mental version of LinkedIn—"you run a gaming company in an incubator office space in San Jose."

My memory jogs. "Big Boss Games?" I add.

"That's us," Evan says.

"You guys are sort of like WordPress for video games, right?" Kyle asks.

Evan flashes a smile. "Yeah, you could say that. It's exciting. We're crushing it right now. Feeling the growing pains a bit, but that's all part of world domination."

"Growing pains?" Kyle asks with some hesitation, but he seems genuinely interested.

"You know, getting the right people on the bus, trimming the fat, that sort of thing. I mean, do we really need a beer tap in the break room? We've lost some of the frat-house fun of a start-up, and we're trying to be a serious company now, you know?"

I nod. "Oh yeah." Boy did I know.

"Dude, I'd come work for you right now if you keep the beer tap," Kyle says, laughing. "Not that I need it." We all laugh.

The lights blink, a signal to take our seats. As I turn around, there at our table sits the guy from seat 18C. I read his name tag—Jack Angel.

"You look familiar," he says with a smile. "I'm Jack." He stands and shakes my hand.

"I'm Chad. I had no idea that was you; we could've visited. I'm sorry I . . ."

"Impossible," he interjects. "I don't think Elizabeth had seen another human in months. I enjoy talking to people, but wow! We'll have plenty of time to visit this weekend. I'm glad you're in my group."

As we take our seats, a voice from the center of the room commands our attention. The voice is attached to a tall guy, at least six-foot three. He casually walks to the stage and turns toward us.

4

THE NORTH STAR

"Hi, I'm Mark Rollins, founder of this retreat," the tall guy says, owning the stage. "Welcome! We're so glad you're here. I believe this weekend can change you and your company as much as anything else in the world. Here's how it'll work.

"First of all, we've carefully selected a handful of leaders to be teamed up with you. They're sitting with you right now. These are amazing entrepreneurs who will be your coaches for the weekend. They each come from different career disciplines, and each is uniquely qualified to guide you through this retreat. I hope you'll take the time to get to know them."

We all glance around the table, giving polite smiles and nods.

"Second, some of you have already asked where to find the agenda. You won't. Seriously, feel free to ask for one, but we'll ignore you." We all laugh.

"We like to keep you guessing, slightly off-balance. You need to know that this is not a typical leadership retreat. We're more interested in diving deep into our stories than we are in teaching seminars. Over the next few days, we want you to take a good hard look at yourself. We've found that is when true personal growth takes place. Without genuine self-awareness, there's just no way you can reach your true potential."

I shifted a bit. I had a feeling this retreat wasn't going to be like the hundreds of other business events I'd been to.

Mark continued. "When it comes to self-awareness, let me also say that there are lots of things that inform our story and are part of discovering our authentic self. That includes our backstory, our individual values and even our spiritual journeys. We want you to bring your whole self - your mind, body, and spirit. To that point, please know that this retreat is safe place, regardless of your expression of faith or lack of it."

"Last, know that we have carefully curated the attendees of the retreat so we can maximize your experience. We believe there are others here who can encourage you, spark new ideas, and hopefully help you take your leadership beyond where it's been. But to get the most out of this time, you'll have to engage authentically with those around you."

The entire room nods. I pull out my smartphone and begin making a list of the themes I'm hearing. I type *awareness* and *authenticity*.

Mark continues, "So hang on, here we go. What I'm about to share with you is what I consider to be the single greatest secret to my success as an investor and as a businessman over the past thirty years." On the screen behind him, a light emerges right in the center.

"I call it the North Star."

I can't even guess what he's about to say. I'm usually skeptical of any "single greatest secret" because it always feels like a sales pitch. But something about Mark's tone puts me at ease.

"There are two things that should drive the modern-day entrepreneur: results and passion. Without passion, an entrepreneur is dead in the water. Without results, there is no way to measure success or failure, so failure is the likely outcome. In both business and life, we are driven by these two forces.

"When a leader is focused primarily on results, that's what I call the *mercenary mind*. The symbol of the mercenary is the sword. Now I know the word *mercenary* and the image of a sword conjure up scenarios of someone willing to do anything, ethical or not, for the almighty dollar. But that's not what I'm talking about here, at least not entirely. I want to redefine the word.

"Yes, according to the Oxford English dictionary, a mercenary is 'a person primarily concerned with making money at the expense of ethics.' Considering that ethics are foundational to any truly successful leader, we're going to replace the word *ethics* with the word *feelings*. The war this mercenary is fighting is generally recognized in our society as a just war. For now, let's not argue about whether capitalism is just or not. Let's assume it is just because it is the engine to economic growth. Later in this retreat we will begin the conversation about whether or not change to this economic system is on the horizon. I believe the existing power structures are going to evolve because of new technology and a growth in consciousness, but that is a conversation for later.

"For now, understand that the mercenary mind is focused on results, the financial bottom line, and not on the feelings of the people who are needed in achieving those results. The mercenary mind values things like execution and economics over everything else. But remember our definition of the mercenary is that this person is achieving these results without lying, cheating, or stealing. I understand this word is rather shocking and unsettling, which is the very reason I'm using it—to wake you up to reality. If you don't know how to beat your competition, your organization will die, plain and simple. There are winners and losers. This is the society we live in.

"Our capitalistic society is more brutal than many of us might be willing to admit. Hang with me here. Remember, the economics of Adam Smith is about the concept of limited resources and scarcity. This capitalistic economy is driven on the notion that everyone is doing what is in their own best interest. It's a 'survival of the fittest' mentality. In my experience, most boards of companies don't spend near as much time talking about culture as they do dissecting the financial results and related metrics that they believe influence the financial returns. This is a reality, so to survive in our economic system you'd better know how to pick up the sword and swing it effectively."

My gut tightens as my mind flashes back to the conference room with Marcus and Co. That's a part of what they were telling me, that I wasn't mercenary enough. What is going on?

"The mercenary uses the weapons of wise action and precise execution to make the most money. If someone in the organization is not a solid performer, the mercenary is willing to quickly make a change for the economic good of the organization. What is good for the organization is more valued than what is best for the individual. The feelings of the person who is fired matters but is not most important. I'm sure you have heard the adage, '*This is not personal; it's just business.*' The mercenary will find a weakness in the competition and expose it . . . even unto the competitor's death. In fact, you hope the competitor dies. No mercy."

Toward the front of the room, someone who looks a little

disturbed asks, "What's the other one? What's the other mindset that drives great leaders?'"

Mark takes a breath for dramatic effect. "The other motivation is what I call the *missionary mind*. The symbol we use for this mindset is the heart. For the missionary, the mission matters over the money and purpose far outweighs profit. Passion, culture and vision are the prime drivers for the missionary."

Even as Mark is talking, my mind races back to Marcus in the boardroom and my conversation with Eric in the car. The words *missionary* and *mercenary* echo in both of those situations. The universe, it seems, is trying to tell me something.

I refocus on Mark's words: "purpose far outweighs profit."

Purpose over profit. I naturally like that idea. Even though I've never put a name to it, that's how I always try to lead. In fact, it is partly why it has been so hard for me to let good people go, even when it's clear they no longer are a fit with the company's needs.

Mark continues, "No question, the missionary mind can be powerful and transformational. As stated by an ancient philosopher, '*Without vision the people perish.*' Money will never be enough to give our lives meaning. Deep within our DNA we desire a deeper purpose for our lives. We really are designed to advance the cause of humanity and to be co-creators of the universe.

"Without vision the people perish." —King Solomon

"In order to make money, an organization needs a

26

mission and purpose. But without money, the mission will never be fully realized."

Mark steps to a whiteboard and writes the two words: *missionary* and *mercenary*.

I have to admit, even with Mark's welcoming tone, his whole pitch sounds a bit too simplistic to me. Apparently, I'm not the only one.

Alex from the Barbarian Group, who is sitting at my table, asks loudly, "So that's the secret? That there are two competing values or minds that CEOs must choose between? C'mon." The way she says it is all business.

Mark smiles. "No. These are not two mindsets you must choose between. This isn't one or the other, good versus bad. If you commit to learning how, you can be both. And to truly thrive as a leader and to be sustainable in today's competitive world, you must be both. As humans, we naturally find a missionary outlet for our passion and a mercenary way to survive. Because we all have a deep-seated need for self-actualization, most people find some outlet for their 'inner missionary.' It might be a hobby or politics or religion. Because we all need to eat, we have a mercenary path as well. But there is no best side, or one side or the other—both matter.

"That means most of us live in the tension between our inner missionary and our inner mercenary. But there are those few people who have discovered how to combine the missionary and mercenary, the heart and the sword.

"When that happens, the power of focus is greater than the sum of its parts, creating entrepreneurs of truly exponential impact. These Thrivers are able to focus their time on what they find life-giving while getting paid for it. This is probably the greatest value of being an entrepreneur. Time, our most valuable resource, is not wasted. One's time is spent on one's passion, which allows more to be accomplished during a lifetime. Let me say that once again for emphasis—this focus allows you to accomplish more of what you were created to be and to do in your lifetime.

"Thrivers have discovered the secret of being both a missionary and a mercenary at the same time. This is called a non-dualistic mindset. Think of King Arthur's Knights of the Round Table. They were noble and exhibited great character, but they also knew how to fight. Now careful, or you'll hear me talking some tough and tender, leather and lace approach. I'm not. I'm talking about a fierceness that runs through both of these ways of thinking and is vital to both."

Mark walks to a second whiteboard and draws a large vertical line with the word *mercenary* along it. Then, beginning at the bottom of the vertical line, he draws a large horizontal line with the word *missionary* along it.

"You're familiar with the right-brain versus left-brain conversations?" Mark asks. "Left-brained people are usually defined as more analytical and methodical, like mercenaries. And right-brained people are thought to be more artistic, empathetic, and intuitive, much like the missionary is. The big difference is that we tend to think of most people as being either right-brained or left-brained. In our case, what we're aiming for is the integration of both missionary and mercenary mindsets at the same time, understanding that holding both and learning how to live well in the tension are essential to thriving.

"From the time we are young, most of us are programmed to believe that we are one or the other. Here's an example. Several decades ago, NASA created a simple test to measure potential creativity of astronaut candidates. After *Apollo 13*, we realized the importance of creativity and innovation during missions.

"As it turns out, only 15 percent of potential astronauts passed the test. But here's where it gets interesting. A whopping 98 percent of five-year-olds passed the exact same test. Why? This is because we tend to believe about ourselves what we've been conditioned to believe. Our identities and true selves can get lost over time."

This surprises me at first, but the more I think about it, it makes sense. When we're young, we haven't had enough negativity in life to reinforce our fears or doubts or limitations.

Mark must have read my face. He looks directly at me, glances at my name tag, and says, "Chad, do you have any thoughts about this?"

It catches me by surprise. "Uh, well, actually, yes. Historically in business, I haven't often struggled with negativity. My problem is the opposite. I've always been too optimistic—at least until recently. Too much blue sky for my own good."

Mark is totally dialed in to me. "What do you mean by that?"

"Well, for example, I always thought we would develop and sell our products faster than we actually did. That got us into trouble at Sensors Everywhere because we built our expense budget based on projected revenue, a forecast that we've never achieved. But the Internet of Things is a wild west. Security and scalability issues that weren't a problem at first began to swallow us alive. That eventually got me into a recent meeting with an investor where I had no leverage."

"I can totally sympathize with that, Chad," Mark adds, "but just because you had a rough season or difficult meeting doesn't change your true identity."

5

WHO ARE YOU?

Mark turns to draw a line beginning where the first two lines meet and extends the line to the far top-right corner of the drawing.

"This is those two traits, the missionary and the mercenary, coming together. That is what it takes to be a Thriver. Every one of you in this room falls somewhere on this graph.

"I'd like to give a modern-day example of how these two mindsets can work together in an integrated way. I realize that the Millennial Generation has been beat up a lot, and some of this is deserved. But I'm excited to see that over the last few years, more and more young and socially conscious entrepreneurs are realizing the importance of both mission and money. In addition to leading companies that are vision-driven, we're now starting to see a brand-new kind of entrepreneur, a person who understands that all sustainable organizations in the future must embrace the importance of social impact. This is a new kind of awareness that is essential moving forward.

"These are founders and leaders who are committed to finding ways to be socially conscious while staying true to the economic engines that power our industries. We will talk about this more later, but to be successful in the next generation of entrepreneurship, the marketplace will demand that we not only know how to beat the competition with superior products or services, but we'd better have a strategy to give back and care for our communities—for humanity.

"The Millennial Generation, which soon will dominate the workforce, is demanding that all corporations contribute in some way to social good. Their influence is reshaping a new type of economy that requires social responsibility. Some of these entrepreneurs demonstrate their commitment to social impact by giving a percentage of corporate profits to charitable causes or by actively participating in serving their local communities. Other such entrepreneurs actually make the social impact component a core function of their business purpose.

"Think about it. In corporate America, entrepreneurship is the engine that drives capitalism, and capitalism is the engine that drives our economic system. Describing our business-driven economy, renowned economist Milton Friedman once stated that 'the social responsibility of business [is] to increase its profits.' This absolute mindset will no longer work in the new human economy. Early American commerce was driven by the agrarian economy; then in the 1920s our country moved into the industrial economy. Since the advent of the computer age, we have become a knowledge economy. With the exponential growth that has come with the digital revolution and the automation of so many jobs, this new generation is leading us into the human economy.

"Accordingly, the social impact requirement on entrepreneurship is changing, which means that Adam Smith's invisible hand is taking on a new shape because of the demands of the Millennial Generation. It's more of an open hand now. Millennials are voting with their job choices and the dollars they spend—or just as important, the dollars they don't spend.

"The good news for the mercenary is that some studies have suggested that socially responsible companies outperform their market competitors by more than ten times, which makes sense given the economic power and demand of this new generation. They want to buy from socially conscious organizations.

"Corporations must be about both making money and improving lives in our communities and our world. This is no longer a 'good to have' strategy; this is a 'must have' strategy. The social impact entrepreneurs are the leaders who can bring the best of the mercenary and missionary mindsets to every situation. This mindset of entrepreneurship will be necessary to thrive."

Mark pauses to look across the room. I do too and notice he has everyone's attention.

I have to admit this feels a little surreal. I went to a university that had in its motto *Pro Humanitate*, meaning "for humanity." As a young capitalist, I never quite understood what service to our communities and concern for the world had to do with my economics degree, which taught me all about scarce resources and Adam Smith's notion that the engine of our economic system is self-interest. But now I am beginning to get it. What if somehow I could find a convergence of my passion, my job, and doing what is good *for humanity*? If so, I'm in.

"Each of you has what it takes to move closer to being a truly Thriver, one who is able to accomplish both mindsets at the same time—the modern-day version of a heroic knight. In fact, that's the primary reason we selected you. We know that each of you has the capacity to turn your organization into a thriving organization." Mark makes eye contact with as many of us as he can.

"So," he says, "for the next few days, our goal is to help you take at least one big step toward being a thriving, integrative, socially conscious, and successful leader. I promise you, if you determine to get everything you can out of this weekend, you will be well on your way to becoming the sort of leader who will not only find success in your organization, but who'll create a ripple effect of noble legacy for years and years to come.

"Okay, in a few moments, you'll break into groups to get to know each other a bit better. My guess is that each of you would categorize yourself as predominately either a missionary or a mercenary. Let that guide your conversation. Share which you think you mostly are, and why you think that."

Mark pauses and then continues. "Let me say something here. I hope by now you've already realized that this isn't a typical leadership retreat. For starters, we are a lot more concerned about who you are than about what you know. In fact, if the main thing you come out of this retreat with is a greater awareness of yourself, you are well on your way to being a Thriver.

"But for that to happen, you have to be willing to be vulnerable and honest with your team—and yourself. Before you get up and take time with your group, I think it would be good for all of us to relax and calm our minds. I'm going to take us through a very short practice, called mindfulness."

Okay, now we may be crossing the line into too much weirdness, at least for me. I'm not into Eastern religions or New Age stuff. I don't want to be judgmental about how others do things, but this just isn't me.

Mark continues, "This is not about a religious practice or goofy meditation. It's really just about being intentional and focused and truly present."

Is this guy seriously reading my mind? That's freaking bizarre!

"There is proven science behind mindfulness," Mark continues. "Even the Navy SEALs use these practices to calm their minds before a mission. And that's really what's happening this weekend—we are pursuing a mission for our families, our companies, and ourselves. And before we can face our dragons, we have to be focused and relaxed."

Mark looks around the room and takes a deep breath.

"For just one minute, I want you to practice some simple breathing exercises with me. Again, all I'm asking from each of you is one minute. Close your eyes, and focus on your breathing.

"Breathe in through your nose for four seconds. Hold

your breath for four seconds. Breathe out through your nose for four seconds. And then again, breathe in, hold your breath for four seconds, breathe out. And repeat."

Okay, I want to have an open mind. I promised Maggie that I would try to get as much as I could out of this retreat, weird or not. So I begin the mindfulness exercise, but all I can think about is how stupid I feel and how this retreat could be a big waste of time. What will they do next? Yoga poses?

"If your mind starts focusing on anything other than your counting and your breathing, just calmly bring it back," Mark says.

I try to focus only on my breathing.

"Let those other thoughts that come up just flow on by. This may not be easy for some of you, but don't beat yourself up. This takes practice, which takes time. Let's all keep silent and continue with the exercise."

After a long minute, I open my eyes and have to admit, I feel calmer, more focused, and a bit less worried. Huh.

Light music fills the air, and the six of us look up awkwardly at each other for a moment.

Then Jack stands up.

"Okay, I don't know about you guys, but I think I've had about as much of this room as I can stand today. What do you say we take it outside? I've asked one of the staff to get a fire ready for us."

We all look at each other.

"I've got local beer and some pretty amazing scotch waiting for us."

"I'm in," Maya says.

"Me too," Evan adds.

We all laugh and give our approval and then head out to find a fire already burning, ringed with logs cut as stools. After grabbing a beer, I sit down next to Alex, and we wait for what's next.

Jack holds a glass of Glenlivet and sits down opposite of me, looking around at all of us. He pauses for a few seconds. The fire flickers, the stars shine overhead, the leaves of the aspen trees flutter in the night.

Man, these guys really know how to set an extravagant table.

"I want you each to know how honored I am to be able to spend a few days with you. I really hope we can get to know one another in real and meaningful ways. I am absolutely convinced that this weekend can be the catalyst to transform your life, but I know the only way for that to happen is for us to be open and authentic and vulnerable with each other.

"I want to know a little bit of each of your stories. But I also want you to know mine. I can't expect you to share deeply if I am not willing to do it first. So, let me tell you a bit about myself, and then I'll ask each of you to tell us at least some of your story. And maybe then tell us if you see yourself as more of a missionary or a mercenary. That way we can say we've done our homework for the night."

I like this guy. He has an easy and honest way about him. I take a drink from my beer as Jack begins.

"Here's the short version of my story. I grew up in a small town in California. My dad worked hard, but he always struggled to pay the bills. Life was hard on him, and he took it out on me and my brother. He never physically abused us, but no doubt he did emotionally. He often told me that I would never accomplish much in life. Maybe he thought this was a good way to motivate me, and perhaps it did in some cruel way. Movies were my escape. I devoured them. I memorized them. And I was fortunate enough to study them in college as a part of UCLA's Writers' Program.

"For years, I worked as an ad copy man, writing novels in my spare time. Then I was hired to write a screenplay and ended up in Hollywood. I worked my way up from staff writer to screenwriter to director and then to executive producer. I finally got my big break on a major studio film, and it flopped. Not a minor flop but an epic, in-every-newspaper-in-the-country sort of flop. Within a few months, I was fired by the studio. I couldn't get a job in movies to save my life. I remember I was out of work, my girlfriend left me, and I was literally living in my car. I really believe I had a nervous breakdown from the stress I was feeling."

Jack takes a sip from his glass. I am shocked at his vulnerability. Authenticity is so inviting. I can feel some of my guard coming down.

"So, what happened?" Evan asks.

"After a lot of therapy and reflection, I eventually got a job writing business pitches for a start-up venture capital firm in San Francisco. As the company grew, I grew along with it. It didn't take long for me to discover that a lot of the principles I'd learned in the movie business applied in very similar ways to the world of entrepreneurship. Little by little, with the help of one of the older partners, I learned to face my own 'shadow self,' which is to say the positive and negative things about me that I'd hidden away because of the pain of my past.

"That mentor also taught me how to swing a sword in business, and I even began to invest in a few of the companies our firm was involved with. I found the companies that I thought had the best stories, and it worked. Eventually I became a partner in the company and then went on to start my own private equity fund. The rest, I suppose, is history."

"What does that make you?" Alex asks. "A missionary or a mercenary?"

Jack smiles. "You remembered our homework. I think I'm mostly a missionary. I've had to learn to be a mercenary, but it's been one of the great joys of my life. I've discovered the miracle that happens when the two converge. I'm grateful to be able to wield a sword while still living from my heart, but honestly, I constantly have to course-correct and recalibrate or I tend to fall back too much into my missionary ways without enough thought about making the venture sustainable.

"There's one other thing I need to share with you, which is hard for me to talk about. During the heyday of my career, I prioritized my work over my family. Both my marriage and my relationship with my kids suffered—a lot. Praise God my marriage somehow has survived, but there is plenty of carnage. I now try to demonstrate to my wife that she is my first priority and what matters to me the most, and I want to be intentional to spend quality time with my three adult children. I have a lot of regrets. But I am all about redemptive stories. That is why I volunteer to be a coach at this retreat. I want to help others avoid some of the land mines I stepped on."

Something about Jack pulls me in. I want to hear more from this guy. And now I want to tell him all about my life, my marriage, my kids, and the decision I am faced with after that boardroom drama. I decide right then and there to make a point to pick Jack's brain a bit more and share more of my story. I want whatever it is he has. There is a peace about him. He feels safe.

"Oh, and I almost forgot," Jack continues, "I've been

married for thirty years to the same beautiful woman, and her name is Eliza. On any given weekend, you'll find me on a tennis court with a racket or in a river with a fly rod. There you have it, that's me. Now, how about a quick intro from each of you, and then tell us which you think you *mostly* are— missionary or mercenary."

6

HI, MY NAME IS…

Alex is quick to start. "Hi, everyone. My name is Alex Miller. I'm the CEO of the Barbarian Group, a consultancy specializing in high tech. I'm not ready to expose my soul like Jack just did, but I grew up in Atlanta and moved to San Fran"—she nods at Jack—"as soon as I could, and I never left. I was married, but that didn't last long. No question, I'm a mercenary through and through. Come to think of it, I imagine that's why my marriage didn't last," she says with a sly grin as she takes a sip from her glass.

We all laugh awkwardly.

"To be honest, I've no interest in being a missionary. It's just not how I'm geared—I am very competitive. I work hard and manage our business to maximize my time and our clients' money. I don't like to waste time with things that make people feel good but don't build the company. My job is to make money, plain and simple. I suppose that's my noble cause, and it's working!"

Alex raises her glass and takes a drink.

"Wow, Alex, thanks for your honesty," Jack says. "I've read a lot about the Barbarian Group. You haven't just cracked the glass ceiling; you've shattered it. In case you didn't know," he says to the rest of us, "the Barbarian Group, which focuses on cybersecurity and other emerging technologies, is currently trending to be one of the most successful start-up venture capital firms in the country this year."

"I've got a question for you, Alex," I say, a bit surprised that I'm jumping in so quickly.

"Sure, shoot," she says.

"I saw an article about you in *ReThink Magazine*. The interviewer asked you to name one thing most people wouldn't know about you, and you said it was the fact that you're writing a novel. Really? A novel?"

Alex blushes. And she looks down, just slightly.

"Well, yes. You've caught me off guard, to be honest. It's really just more like journaling, but yes, I'm writing a novel. I've always loved writing, and I think I'm actually pretty good at it. What I wouldn't give on some days to quit the corporate gig and write full time."

There is a short silence.

"So, why not?" I ask.

"Are you kidding? And miss out on the payoff? The big pop? I've worked hard and I'm finally pulling in an amazing salary, but my stock is really where the value is. When I finally do retire, I'll be doing pretty well for myself."

"Sounds a lot like golden handcuffs to me," Jack says.

Everyone laughs. Everyone except Alex.

"Well, I'd love to read what you've written if you ever put it out there for the world to see," Jack says.

"Don't hold your breath." Alex finds her grin again.

Next to Alex is a striking-looking woman I guessed might

have been from India. She looked to be in her twenties and had bright eyes and an unforgettable smile. Just seeing her smile makes me want to smile in return.

"I'd love for you all to meet Maya," Jack says. "Maya is an artist. She's not exactly the typical attendee of the Entrepreneur's Retreat, but once I saw her work and read her application, I knew instantly that she needed to be here with us."

Maya smiles at each of us. It is obvious that she isn't as comfortable with groups as Alex.

"Honestly, I'm just grateful to be here," Maya says.

"So, how would you describe yourself most of the time?" Jack asks.

"Ever hear of a starving artist? Well, that's me. I guess you'd call me the ultimate missionary," she says, looking at Jack like she wants to get out of this discussion.

"So, Maya," Alex chimes in, "tell us more about the work you do. I'd love to hear more about your story."

Maya smiles awkwardly.

"Well, even as a child, I knew I wanted to be an artist. I was in junior high when my parents moved our family to the states and I struggled a bit to fit in. Art was my refuge and a place I could truly express myself and make sense of the new culture and people around me. It sort of became an obsession. When other kids were playing sports or out on dates, I was up to my elbows in oil paints and sculpting clay."

I loved the way Maya seemed so passionate about art. I sort of envied her.

"It's where I feel most alive," she continued. "I think I've always just seen things differently. Not that my parents saw it the same way. My dad was a doctor, and all he ever said was that art wasn't a *real career*. Fortunately, I won a national art contest as a senior in high school and was offered a scholarship to a great art school in France."

"Did you go?" I ask.

"I did. I spent four years in Paris and fell in love with sculpting. Got pretty good at it, too. I moved back to NYC and started to make a name for myself. One day, I started posting pics of my work on Instagram and even began blogging about my work. A lot of my art tells the story of women in the world struggling with freedom—refugees, trafficked girls, laborers who face horrific working conditions."

As Maya tells her story, all traces of her discomfort disappear. She comes alive, like she just discovered a secret treasure and is so excited to share it with us. She tells us about her artwork, famous people she's worked with, her crusade for freedom, people who have bought her work, and she shares her plans for new work. But then her face turns, and she gets quiet.

"What?" Jack asks.

"But that's where things get weird for me," she says. "That's where things get discouraging."

"What do you mean?" Evan asks. "Sounds to me like you're hitting on all cylinders."

"I'm spending so much on my apartment, my studio, and other living expenses. Even with all the new business, the truth is, I'm broke. Although I think my art is great, apparently others don't think it's worth enough for me to make a living. If I didn't work as a waitress on weekends, I would really be in even deeper trouble financially."

She takes a breath.

"Who am I fooling? Perhaps my father was right after all. This isn't a real job. Not like yours are." I can see the emotion in Maya's face. Her eyes dance darkly in the light of the fire.

44

No one speaks. I can see the pain in Maya's face. The fire circle is suddenly a sacred space. She takes a deep breath.

"My father thinks I'm crushing it. But I'm not. I feel like nothing but a fake, a poser. To tell you the truth, if it weren't for my sister paying for this weekend, I wouldn't be here at all."

She took a deep breath and continued. "As a child, my father would always remind me *the important thing is that mankind should have a purpose in life. It should be something useful. Something good.* Sometimes I wonder if what I do is useful at all."

The important thing is that mankind should have a purpose in life. It should be something useful. Something good. —Ghandi

---

"Maya," Jack says, "Without a doubt, what you do is useful and very important. I've seen your work and based on what you've told me and what I've read about you, you're on a good path. It sounds to me like you've got all the ingredients you need for a really special business and life. Honestly, you're closer to success than you think. All you need is a little coaching."

Maya smiles weakly.

Next, Jack turns to Evan. He jumps right in.

"Hey, everyone! I'm Evan. I've never really thought about the whole missionary/mercenary thing before, at least not in those terms. Honestly, I'm relatively new at my business. I feel like I'm just getting my business legs running at full speed. I own a company that makes engines for video games. We're only four years old, and up till now, I've sort of had to wear all the hats. At first, I guess I was more missionary because I had to be in order to get seed capital and good people. I had to sell the story, you know? But now that we're up and rolling, I've had to set aside the missionary stuff and do the work. I'm all about being a mercenary now, although I'm not entirely sure that's a good thing."

"How'd you get your start?" Kyle asks.

"Well, growing up I was one of those annoying guys who was pretty good at everything. I was QB on our high school football team, and grades and girls came easy to me."

Evan strikes me as pretty arrogant. I mean, is he actually saying this stuff out loud? I mean . . . *good with the girls?* Yikes. But I have to admit, he is sharp—good-looking, smart, articulate, and easygoing. I can't help but think of a young Steve Jobs. I doubt Evan ever questions whether or not he has what it takes to be successful.

"Fortunately," he continues, "video games and computers in general came easy to me, too. I went to MIT, and after graduating I went to work for a pretty influential gaming company. Then, one day I woke up and realized that there was a big opportunity in creating the complex platforms that video games run on. I got a small loan from my parents and an angel round, and I decided to take the leap."

"You quit your job and started this full time?" Jack asks, a bit of a serious look on his face.

"Yeah. All in, you know? I burned the ships and jumped in. Been going a hundred miles an hour ever since. In the words of my hero, I wanted to *put a ding in the universe.*"

"I want to put a ding in the universe." — Steve Jobs

"Good ole' Steve Jobs. So, how's the new company?" Alex asks.

"Gangbusters. I mean, there are days when I wonder how we're even keeping up. I don't sleep much, and I pretty much have a coffee IV hooked up to me all the time. But hey, you guys know the drill . . . gotta do whatever it takes, right?"

"You can sleep when you die," Alex says. We all nod as if there's strength in numbers or something. Jack smiles but doesn't say anything. But I can tell he's thinking something.

Evan continues, "But I do wonder if we are losing our soul as a company in the process." He looks at me and Kyle. "Earlier I was telling some of the guys about the change in our company's culture lately."

"What do you mean?" Jack asks.

"Well, it's just that when we first started, I was obsessed with the culture of our company. We were the type of place where young, socially conscious business people *wanted* to work. We had a vibrant family feel and really focused on giving back to our community, just like Mark talked about tonight."

Evan takes a drink from his beer.

"But as we've grown and taken on investors, I've had to be more serious. I guess you'd call it *more mercenary*. We've cut back on almost everything that doesn't directly impact our bottom line. Our investors demand a lot. We are tight financially, but we are growing quickly."

"You sound like you don't think being a mercenary is a good thing," Alex says.

"I guess I'm just not sure. If I'm being honest, we've left some really great people without work. But they just couldn't grow with us."

Evan pauses for a moment.

"But you know what? I honestly don't really care. We're

47

doing what we need to do to thrive, and I'm not going to apologize for that. If people can't figure out how to adapt, that's their problem. I've got to look out for myself and my company first. Hell yeah, I'm a mercenary. Write that down —Evan is a mercenary."

He's got guts—that's for sure. But somehow I'm not convinced. And I'm not certain he is, either.

"And Kyle, how about you?" Jack asks, moving the conversation away from Evan.

"Oh, I'm definitely a missionary. We are all about social impact. I guess that's why I'm running Splash. We're a nonprofit that helps entrepreneurs in foreign countries start and grow micro-businesses to purify and distribute water. And by the way, we're nonprofit in the truest sense of the word. We haven't made a profit since our inception. But I guess in my case, it's better for me to be a missionary than a mercenary."

"Why do you say that?" Jack asks.

"I don't know. I just think that since we're a nonprofit, the missionary mindset seems more appropriate."

Jack frowns. "Kyle, I want to reiterate what Mark said, that the mercenary mindset he defined is not a negative one. Quite the opposite. I think words like *accountability*, *execution*, and *operational excellence* have been given a bad rap."

"I love those words!" Alex chimes in. Everyone laughs.

Jack laughs, too. "And I think we all need to learn to respect those words as much as we do words like *vision, heart*, and *mission* if we want to have sustainable companies. In fact, you need to realize that all nonprofits are in competition for those donor dollars, which makes it a very competitive space. Your mission, therefore, must be compelling. So, tell us a bit more of your story, Kyle."

"Okay. Let's see, a bit more background on me. I was

born in Guatemala. My parents were both missionaries there, in the truest sense of the word. I actually had an amazing childhood and don't remember any lack, but I know my parents survived only because of the people in the States who supported them."

He pauses for a moment. "Now that I think of it, that's probably where I get some of my missionary disposition.

"Anyway, after high school I moved to the States. I'm an LSU grad with degrees in economics and philosophy. With those majors, you'd think I would be a good mercenary *and* missionary. After college, I met my now-wife Sophie on a humanitarian trip to Uganda. She was there with the Peace Corps. I once heard Mother Theresa say that *peace begins with a smile,* so you might say we decided to find a solution to world peace together. Anyway, it was on that trip that we realized the plight of so much of the continent.

"Peace begins with a smile." —Mother Theresa

"Sophie and I decided we wanted to invest our lives to help others who were less fortunate, specifically in developing countries. We strive to find ways to use their natural talents to solve real problems, while at the same time creating self-sufficient microeconomic solutions. Water seemed like the obvious first thing to tackle. Thus, Splash Inc. was born. That was ten years ago. Honestly, I had no idea that running a business was going to be this hard."

"Sounds like a recipe for a killer social impact organization," Alex says. "Why not make money *and* help people?"

Kyle pauses. "I've never really thought of Splash that way. I don't know . . . I just don't know that I have the instinct or skills to run that sort of organization. I'm a pretty easygoing guy. I just don't have the cutthroat personality that I think a for-profit company needs.

"No offense to you guys," he says, looking at Alex and Evan. "I really do respect what you do, but I just don't think I'm cut out for it. I don't think I have the sort of nerve needed to lead like that."

Kyle and I have more in common than I thought. We both have big ideas we are passionate about, and we both tend to lean more toward vision and mission than implementation and execution. *People over profit.*

"That's sort of my story too, in a sense," I add. I really am not ready to bear my soul to everyone, but I am the only one left.

"My name's Chad, and I run a technology company called Sensors Everywhere. We combine cutting-edge AI technology with standard networks and sensors."

"Sounds like science fiction," Maya says.

"Good timing!" Evan adds. "With the Internet of Things, networks and sensors are the place to be. So here's an idea for you…"

Jack makes like an NFL ref. "Time out. Hold on. We'll have lots of time to talk more. How'd you get into that, Chad? You just woke up one morning and decided to get into sensors?"

"Well, not exactly." I pause for a second, deciding how much to tell them.

"I grew up in a pretty well-to-do family. My grandfather owned a company that manufactured transistors for some of the earliest computers. Out of college, I jumped into the family business and worked there until about ten years ago. I worked in executive roles for several tech companies before I started Sensors Everywhere."

"Which type of leader are you?" Alex asks.

I pause for a moment, but I know the answer.

"Well, I actually think I'm more of a missionary than a mercenary even though I'd like to think of myself as a kick-ass-and-take-numbers sort of leader. But that's just not me. I sort of wish it was, but it's not."

"You wish you were more of a mercenary? What makes you wish that?." Jack asks.

"I don't know exactly. I just think more mercenary would allow me to be more decisive and aggressive when I need to be."

I turn to Alex, determined to deflect the attention from my story. "Sounds like you're the most mercenary in the group, Alex. What sparked the mercenary thing in you?"

She pauses for a moment.

"As long as I can remember, I've been more of a mercenary," Alex continues. "I've always been a type A, hard-charging person. In college I was an overachiever, and in business I feel like I've had to fight to make it to where I am."

Kyle jumps in. "I do love the idea of rethinking what it means to make a social impact but not always struggling so much financially. I've just always thought I had to either be a for-profit corporation or a not-for-profit organization. I've never put them together as a both/and. But why not?"

"You know," Alex says, "I'd love to figure that out, too. Now, don't get me wrong. I love making money, and I'm darned good at it. But I wonder if there are ways for our company to make an impact on the world, to improve lives while we kick butt in business at the same time. I've got to admit that if that's what it takes to attract the smartest millennials like Mark said, I've gotta figure it out!"

~

THE SIX OF US spend the next hour getting to know each other more, and then Jack reaches down and picks up a small metal box that was placed near his seat.

"Let me just say how thankful I am that each of you has chosen to open up as much as you have. The first step in becoming a Thriver is self-awareness. If we aren't aware of our own strengths *and* weaknesses, together with a desire for personal growth, there's simply no way we can become all that we need to be as leaders."

Kyle was nodding. "Reminds me of an old philosophy quote… *the most difficult thing in life is to know yourself.*"

"The most difficult thing in life is to know yourself."
—Thales

He's right. For the past hour, pretty much each of us has opened up about our lives, our deficiencies, and our dreams. I might have been the one who said the least. Still, it was so refreshing to be around people who are willing to dip below the waterline of life.

"Tomorrow we're going to do a really deep dive into ourselves. We're going to take a hard look at where we are as entrepreneurs and begin to chart a path of what it's going to take to get us to become Thriver."

Jack reaches into the little metal box and pulls out a stack of papers and a few pens. He hands them out so that each of us has paper and a pen.

"Here's what we're going to do before we head to our rooms for bed. In a few moments, I want each of you to write down on your paper one or more words that represent what you think is standing between where you are tonight and you being a Thriver.

"But before we do that, I want to tell you about something that has been the core of my personal entrepreneur's philosophy."

7

THERE WILL BE DRAGONS

"In the screenwriting world, there's this framework called '*the Hero's Journey*,'" explains Jack. "It was created by a guy named Joseph Campbell, and it's been used as the basis for almost every successful epic movie in the past fifty years.

"Basically, the Hero's Journey goes something like this:

1. We meet the hero, who has no self-awareness of who he or she actually is.
2. The hero is called to a great adventure but refuses the call.
3. The hero meets a mentor and steps across the threshold.
4. The hero faces tests and meets allies and enemies.
5. The hero prepares for battle.
6. The hero faces his or her greatest fear and temporarily gets the reward.
7. The hero loses his or her prize, goes back for it, dies in some way, and is resurrected.

8. The hero brings the reward home. There is transformation.

"This weekend, we are on the Entrepreneur's Journey. And tonight, I want to invite you on a grand adventure. I have to warn you that it won't be easy and may not go the way you expect, but if you accept the call, I can promise you that your life will change. You will experience more life-giving moments than you've ever imagined."

"Will there be dragons like Mark talked about?" Kyle asks with a smile.

Jack smiles wryly. "Actually, yes. I wish I could say there won't be, but the truth is, there are dragons. I suspect there's one prowling around each of you this very moment. In fact, that's what each of you needs to face before this weekend is up."

"Dragons?" Alex asks a bit skeptically.

"Exactly. Each of you has at least one dragon that's standing between your true potential and where you are today. We want to identify that dragon and begin to devise a plan to slay it. Just imagine what your life and your business could be like if you were able to get rid of whatever is standing in the way of you being the best, fullest, strongest, most passionate version of yourself. That's what this retreat is all about."

I can't exactly explain it, but at this very moment I know for sure that this retreat is about more than me and Sensors Everywhere. It is about my family and my future and my soul. In this moment, something begins to happen in me. It is a sense of expectation for something good. *Hope.*

"The first step in defeating your dragon is giving it a name," Jack says. "Keep in mind that you can have more than one dragon, and each one can have a different name.

For the next few moments, I want you to think deeply about what it is that's keeping you from being a Thriver. And I want you to give it a name or names, write down that word or words on your paper, and then throw it into the fire. Maybe your dragon is *self-doubt* or *your father's expectations*, or it could be *fear of failure* or even *other people's opinions.* Maybe you've believed something untrue about yourself for so long that you've decided to accept it.

"Just write it down and then, when you're ready, toss it into the fire. When you do that, what you're saying is that you're willing to accept this call to adventure and begin the Entrepreneur's Journey."

And then Jack falls quiet. No one says a word.

All I can hear is the sound of the fire crackling and the leaves rustling above our heads. After a few moments, Maya turns away from the fire. I can tell she is hiding her face from us. Alex has her head down so we can't see her. Evan is sitting expressionless. Oddly, it is the most vulnerable he's been so far. Kyle is staring into the fire.

Suddenly, this is getting real.

My mind is racing. For a moment, it is like I am bouncing back and forth in time to several moments from my past.

I remember being twelve years old, hunting with my grandfather. I have a deer in my sight, but I can't pull the trigger.

I remember being sixteen years old at the high school dance. I am standing next to the girl of my dreams, but I can't get myself to ask her to dance.

I remember being twenty-five. My boss has asked me to lunch and given me an opportunity to tell him why I should be a senior manager. I freeze.

The final image in my head is the boardroom, just yesterday.

There is something common to all these thoughts, what seems a general theme of my life. I'm not totally sure how to describe it, just a state of generalized fear and anxiety. I fear for my business, my kids, my wife, my health, my finances . . . this list can go on and on. This is no way to live a good life.

That's it. For the first time in my life, I recognize the voice in my head, the constant chatter and self-talk that has been accusing me and mocking me and planting doubt and fear in me my entire life. The voice that constantly taunts that my best days are behind me, that I don't have what it takes to be successful in business or in life. The fearful thoughts are relentless.

It is my own cruel voice. That is my dragon. I hate that voice. It constantly beats the shit out of me. For a moment, I literally feel like I can't breathe. I struggle to focus as I hold the paper.

I pick up the pen and write some words on the paper. I fold the paper and hold it in my hands. I look up. Kyle is standing now, still staring at the fire, looking intently at a spot where a paper is burning. Maya is standing too, with tears gleaming from her eyes. I watch her throw her paper into the fire.

My hands are trembling a little. But I do it.

As I stand there, the paper unfolds, and for a moment I can read the words I have listed. I don't want to leave anything out.

Self-doubt.

Fear.

My internal critic.

I watch the paper burn. We all do. Each of us has named our dragons and thrown them into the fire. The moment is spiritual. We have each made a choice. We have each decided to cross the threshold.

~

AFTER A LONG MOMENT, Jack says, "Well, it's getting late, team. I think it's safe to say that tonight was important for each of us. As you make your way back to your rooms, remember what you put into the fire. If you think tonight was an important step, just wait for tomorrow."

I look at my watch. It's nearly 10 p.m. We've been sitting around the fire for almost three hours, and the time has flown by. I honestly cannot remember a time when I was as excited or as energized by a conference or seminar as I am tonight. Something is different here. I feel both challenged and affirmed. I am invited to share my flaws without any feeling of shame. This is a safe place. I am excited, and maybe a bit nervous, to see what tomorrow holds for us.

Jack dismisses the group, and we all gather our things and begin to make our way back toward the cabins. As the others walk, I hang back a bit. I want to talk to Jack.

"Jack, I just want to apologize for the way I treated you on the plane. I really didn't mean to ignore you . . . I just had no idea who you were. And I was sort of in a bit of an emotional funk."

He waves me away. "Chad, don't even think twice. I'm really glad you're on this team, and I'm looking forward to hearing more of your story in the next few days."

"I'd love that," I say. "I'm really hoping that I can get some time with you while we're here. I'm facing some tough decisions back at home, and I could really use some advice."

Jack turns to me. "Chad, I'd be thrilled to spend some time getting to know you and hearing what's going on with you. But you need to know that even more than your company, I'm interested in *you*. I want to know who you are, what you care about,

58

and why you are here. I sense that you have something special in you just waiting to emerge. And I'm really hoping this weekend can be a big catalyst for you, your family, and your business."

"Thanks, Jack."

"I'm all in with you, Chad. It's going to be a great few days. Now, get some sleep, and I'll see you in the morning."

With that, I find my way back to my room. I lie awake for what seems like at least an hour, playing over the events of the very long day. Then, what feels like a moment later, I awake. It's 5 a.m.

My mind begins tumbling around in a million different directions, jumping around from idea to idea. Our fireside conversation has me thinking in directions I haven't in years. This concept of becoming more self-aware feels important. I need to get up and clear my head. I slip on my running shoes and find one of the several trailheads scattered around the property.

The altitude here is 9,100 feet, so I am feeling a little of that Rocky Mountain high. The views are spectacular, and I am excited about going on a run. But the air is thin up here, so I need to be wise about how far I go and careful about firmly planting my feet in this rugged terrain. Staying hydrated is also a good idea. As I think about it, this sounds like a good metaphor for the non-dualistic entrepreneur — have fun *and* be wise.

I feel conflicted about what mindset motivates me. On one hand, the vision and mission of the missionary resonates with me, but I also understand the importance of being a mercenary when it comes to tough decisions. For as long as I can remember, I've loved strategy and the thrill of the fight, but I also love getting people to be part of something big. Even as a kid with my first garage sale, I was the guy taking charge and cutting deals, but I did it by creating something people wanted to be part of.

What's nagging at me is the fact that I know I need to find a way to possess both the missionary and the mercenary mindset at the same time—and to be good at both. If I'm honest, sometimes it seems like the missionary-minded guys I know are weak and the mercenary leaders I know are mean. Now, I'm beginning to think that maybe I've been misjudging them all along.

I even recall a saying from my Sunday school class when I was a kid, something about *'as shrewd as a snake and as innocent as a dove.'* There is an *and* in that saying rather than an *or* that connects the two. I think that is the first time I have thought about it in that way. Holding both certainly is a non-dualistic concept.

"Therefore be as shrewd as snakes and as innocent as doves."
—Jesus

My mind keeps pulling me back to the fire. Even as I run, I can see the words on my paper. Well, at least I know what my dragon is—my own negative, chattering voice. The more I think about it, the more I begin to think of times that I've listened to that voice and allowed it to shape me into a one-sided leader.

If I could slay that dragon and learn to live from both sides of my true self, what would happen? If I learned to dismiss self-doubt and fear and stood confidently for what I believed in, what would the rest of my days look like?

There is a lot to digest.

8
_____

YOU ARE NOT YOUR THOUGHTS

I'm early for the first session of the day. As I walk in, I see Kyle filling up his coffee cup in the back of the room. Kyle seems to light up when he notices me.

"Hey, Chad!" Kyle says as he walks across the room. "Today is going to be a great day."

I smile. I really like Kyle. His positivity spills out all over everyone, but his joy? It's contagious. Kyle takes a seat next to me just as the session is beginning. A few moments later, Jack and the others join us.

"How'd you all sleep?" Mark asks.

We all respond with variations of "slept well," "went to bed way too late," and "tossed and turned all night."

"I think it's safe to say that last night's session and our conversations were challenging and formative, to say the least," Kyle says. "It sure did get me thinking."

"That's great to hear," Mark says. "I really enjoyed watching you all get to know each other. That's one of the biggest takeaways of this weekend experience—the relationships you'll forge."

Mark moves to the center of the stage again and takes a deep breath.

"I suppose you know what we're going to do next," he says.

"Breathe in, breathe out!" someone shouts. We all laugh.

"You got it. Okay, let's begin our time with another mindfulness exercise. The same thing we did yesterday, but today we are going to try it for two minutes. Some of you may be wondering why we do this as part of an entrepreneur's retreat. I can tell you that in my own life, nothing has been more important than learning to quiet myself from all the noise around me and genuinely being aware and mindful."

He's talking about my dragon.

"Too often we think that our thoughts equate to who we are. I found it so important in my life journey to be aware that just because I have a thought, it doesn't necessarily make it true. What we are doing here is learning to watch our thoughts without always identifying with our thoughts. There is a layer of who we are that is not our thoughts. We call it our conscious self, or some call it our soul.

"When I am able to separate myself from some of the harsh self-talk, monitoring the thoughts as they come and evaluating their truthfulness, I can separate the stimulus from my response. I then have the opportunity to make a choice about what I will do with each thought.

"I also get to choose how the thought should impact me emotionally. Is the thought even true? Because of the importance of this, I practice mindfulness as if my life depends upon it. I believe being able to separate my thoughts from the immediate emotional response is critical to a thriving life. With mindfulness, this ability to monitor our thoughts and not react immediately to them is what we are training our brains to be able to do.

"We are creating some space so that we can appropriately respond rather than immediately react. It does take a lot of practice, so don't beat yourselves up. In fact, it's called contemplative practice. It is hard but worth it. Remember, there is a lot of proven research on the effectiveness of mindfulness. Okay, let's try this again for two minutes—as if your life depends on it!"

I long for freedom from the thoughts that torment me. I am tired of living in fear. I'm going to give this a try, but this time I am going to take it more seriously. 1, 2, 3 . . .

"Thank you for honoring me by trying another mindfulness exercise. Now, let's dig into this session.

"Last night, I gave you the foundational principle of thriving leaders upon which the rest of this weekend will be built. We talked about the importance of holding in as equal value as possible the missionary mind and the mercenary mind. We called that thriving leadership. In order to thrive, it is necessary to know how to both swing a sword and live from our hearts.

"I want to clarify something. This is really important, so I need your undivided attention. While it is true that both mindsets are equally important to survival, thriving leaders start with a mission. Mark clicked a button and quote appeared on the screen behind him.

C. S. Lewis once said, *'Put first things first and we get second things thrown in: put second things first and we lose both first and second things.'*

"Put first things first and we get second things thrown in: put second things first and we lose both first and second things."
—C.S. Lewis

"Leaders who tend to focus on just the money," he continues, "lose the respect and admiration of the followers. People long to be inspired and motivated and want to be a part of a noble cause. While it is true that without enough money the mission will fail, the *money should follow a great purpose.* Just because something must lead does not mean the second thing is less important. For example, ballroom dancers have a lead, but the whole performance needs both dancers equally. The Thunderbirds or the Blue Angels fly in incredible formations. There is a lead plane and the other planes fall in line, but all the planes are necessary for the show.

"Henry Ford once said, 'Business must be run at a profit, else it will die. But when anyone tries to run a business solely for profit . . . then the business must die as well, for it no longer has a reason for existence.' And Walt Disney said it even better: 'We don't make movies to make money; we make money to make more movies.'"

He pauses for a moment. Just for effect.

"Are you with me?"

Heads nod affirmatively as Mark returns to the whiteboard and draws two more lines that divide the graph into four quadrants. Then he runs his finger along the board and taps on each of the four.

"Each of these four quadrants represents a deeper look into what kind of leader you are. After the session last night, I asked each of you to pinpoint where you thought you fell on the graph—closer to the x-axis or the y-axis.

"You'll also see that I've added and labeled each of the four quadrants—*Dreamer, Goldminer, Martyr,* and *Thriver.* Take a look at where you are and see which quadrant you land in."

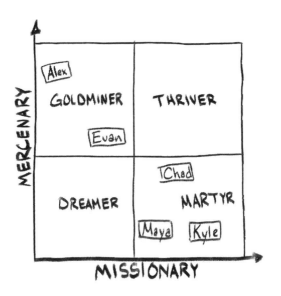

One of the staff walks to our table and hands us each a piece of paper. I can see where Jack put my name, in the bottom-right portion of the diagram, in the Martyr's Quadrant—high in the missionary quotient but lower on the mercenary scale.

Kyle's marker is close to mine, along with Maya's. Alex is squarely in the Goldminer's Quadrant, along with Evan.

Mark walks to the whiteboard and points to the bottom-left quadrant, the point where the two axes meet.

"This is the Dreamer's Quadrant," Mark says. "This is where every organization starts out. This is where ideas are born. It's in the Dreamer's Quadrant that start-ups are fueled and grow. Google, Facebook, Amazon, and Apple all started here."

Mark stops for a moment. He has a look on his face that makes me feel like he is particularly interested in making his next point with a big exclamation point. I can't help but pay close attention.

"I know you all have started your own businesses. I know that many of you have been through seasons of self-doubt.

"We all go through that. But I want you to know that if you have an idea that will make the world a better place, you *owe* it to all of us and to your dream to do everything you can to make it a reality."

Mark pauses for a moment to let that sink in. "Did you hear that? You owe it to your dream to make it a reality. Now, I didn't say that your dream owes you a living. Some of you are running organizations that, frankly, may never make you a personal fortune."

I look over at Maya and try to imagine what she is thinking. Could it be that she never will be able to integrate her job with her passion? I hurt for her and also for Kyle and myself. Our passions may not be sustainable financially.

Mark continues, "Your dreams may not even put food on your table. That doesn't mean you don't pursue and nurture the dream. It simply means you have to change your perspective.

"But please hear this, just because your product or art is not commercially viable at the moment does NOT mean that it is not of significant quality or value. There are numerous examples of works that gained great commercial viability at a later date, even after the death of the artist.

Maya was nodding. Mark was clearly speaking her language.

Think of Vincent van Gogh or Henry Thoreau who never saw the incredible commercial success of their works in their lifetimes. Even copyright law recognizes this reality by granting intellectual property protection 75 years after the death of the author. So don't confuse economic viability with high quality. Sometimes the world has to catch up with the value of your creation.

"It's okay for the dream to be a hobby and not your full-time work. We talked a bit about that last night. It's hard-wired into us to seek out something of meaning to give our time and energy to. I have lots of friends with deep passions for things that don't pay the bills. That doesn't mean they shouldn't do them. It just means they have to be smart about how they do them.

"Regardless of if you are a nonprofit company, a for-profit company, a publicly traded company, a freelancer, or anything in between, no one should stay in the Dreamer's Quadrant. Ultimately, all true entrepreneurs move from the Dreamer's Quadrant to one of these other two"—he points to the upper-left and lower-right quadrants—"which is entirely appropriate. If they don't move, the dream will die.

"Now, you already know this, but it bears repeating. What is not okay is to just talk about your dream without ever doing anything about it. At some point you become a talker instead of a dreamer, and talkers are exhausting, right? Instead of using your energy to talk, take the first step toward making the dream become a reality. It could be a very small step forward, like merely printing some business cards and building a basic website, but that first step is the price of admission to one of the other quadrants. Without real paying customers, by definition you are still in the Dreamer's Quadrant."

He gestures to the lower right quadrant. "Some leaders naturally end up here. This is what I call the Martyr's Quadrant. These leaders tend to be more naturally driven by the missionary mindset. They place a high value on things like vision, mission, purpose, and changing the world. They believe, often somewhat naively, that everyone will surely get behind their noble cause."

I can totally relate to this. That is me, or at least that's who I have become—a missionary. I have a knack for casting a vision and getting people excited about it. I don't mind taking a calculated risk, but I'm not as comfortable with execution and decision-making. And I absolutely hate the idea of ever firing someone.

I've always believed that I have the vision to drive Sensors Everywhere, but I wonder if I've allowed myself to move too far into the Martyr's Quadrant. I think about how I allowed myself to be pushed around in the boardroom the other day. For some reason I'm okay with the word *missionary*, but I bristle at *martyr*. That word is a wake-up call.

Mark continues, "A lot of nonprofits and social enterprises end up in this quadrant. These leaders are the kind of people you love to be around. They usually have an uncanny ability to attract others to their organization, even when they are unable to pay the kind of salaries that others can. The vision and passion they ooze is enough to get great people on the team. Keeping them, however, is the challenge.

"As you'd expect, the weakness with the Martyr's Quadrant is usually the economics. Organizations that camp out here tend to find themselves constantly behind the eight ball when it comes to finances and resources. Cash is usually tight, and these CEOs find themselves continually trying to figure out how to bail themselves out of tough financial situations. Of course, ultimately this isn't sustainable. If you stay here, your organization dies—thus the name Martyr. Sure, you die for a noble cause, but you're still dead."

A hand shoots up. It is a woman who looks to be in her twenties sitting a few tables away from me. Mark stops. "What's your question, Susan?"

"Okay, so I feel like I'm living in the Martyr's Quadrant. But what do you do if you know what you're passionate about, but it just doesn't seem to be able to pay the bills?"

Mark smiles. "There are a lot of implications from your question. Mark Twain once said, 'The two most important days of your life are the day you were born and the day you find out why.' Something very powerful happens when you discover what you were born to do. But too often we confuse our *calling* with our *job*.

"So, Susan, I say this. First, keep your day job. Just because you're passionate about something doesn't mean you should walk away from what keeps food on the table. Keeping your day job will hopefully give you time to determine whether or not your passion can become your living.

"Usually our dreams take time to mature, to blossom, to be pruned into their truest essence. The mission evolves. Perhaps over time that dream can pay the bills, but there certainly are no guarantees. But as long as you are not dependent on that dream paying the bills, then time is on your side.

"A *hobby* is something you love to do that doesn't sustain you and your family financially, and there is no such expectation. In order to change a hobby into something more, you've got to prove the business case. You need to confirm that you have a viable market and paying customers who will sustain you. Some are able to raise seed money to get to a proof of concept. This could be a nonprofit or a Kickstarter project if you want it to be backed by donors. But remember, donation dollars are still subject to competitive pressures. You still have to compete for donor dollars. If this is a for-profit, then you may need to seek angel or seed money, crowdfunding, or a loan. Some must keep their day job and prove the business case over a longer period of time.

"Keep in mind, in the case of a for-profit company, if you

take early seed money, you likely will have to give up a lot of the ownership and perhaps control of your company because early stage companies will have a lower valuation. Whenever you take a dollar of someone's money, there becomes a 'fair' expectation from the investor that you are trying to maximize the value of the organization. Also, there better be some type of 'exit strategy' to monetize their investment. They rightfully want a good financial return on their investment. Depending upon the amount of control the investors have, money can easily become the first thing. At the early stages of a company, if the outside investors have control, I believe money inevitably will become the first thing.

"Taking early funding is a mercenary move. I'm not saying that this is a wrong move; you just need to be aware of and weigh the consequences. Other entrepreneurs who don't want to give up so much equity too early choose to bootstrap their funding, if they can afford it, because they don't want to lose control of the mission."

He has my attention. Is this what is happening with InvestCorp?

"Unfortunately," he continues, "even most business schools teach students to design a business plan that always includes raising rounds of early funding. That isn't always the best move, especially if you value the mission over the money. By taking early money, you may be forced to move into the Goldminer's Quadrant prematurely, which we will talk about shortly. At the same time, a good mercenary in the mix can help to make your business thrive. So I always encourage only taking the amount of money that is necessary to get to the next phase of the company."

I can relate to those last statements. I am on the verge of losing control at Sensors Everywhere, which might not be all bad because I need people around who can sharpen my sword. But will we lose our heart in the process, especially if we bring in a new CEO who doesn't understand or is not passionate about the mission?

"In the case of a nonprofit," Mark continues, "the *investor* is looking at the organization to provide a good ROI. This 'return' may be in the form of metrics that demonstrate the positive social impact of the organization. In fact, all not-for-profit organizations need to think of themselves as if they are for-profit and develop good financial disciplines. Donors of nonprofits don't want their dollars to be wasted."

I look over at Kyle. I can tell his mind is buzzing. I'm anxious to hear what he is thinking, knowing that his company struggles financially. But it sure seems like there are ways for him to turn Splash into a thriving nonprofit organization.

"Leaders in the Martyr's Quadrant," Mark says, "are people who know how to lead from the heart. These leaders show empathy; they are masters at team building and peacemaking. They score high as missionaries but usually fail when mercenary disciplines are needed."

That is my story. I think about the deal with Invest-Corp. That's exactly what has happened. I've been so focused on vision and innovation that I neglected the simple mechanics of economics, key performance indicators, and balanced scorecards. Detailed budgets and schedules drive me crazy. And so does being decisive. Now that I think about it, I know that is mostly because of my own self-doubt.

Do I have what it takes to really swing a sword?

Am I too weak to make the hard calls?

When push comes to shove, will I be able to pull the trigger?

I am beginning to really dislike the fact that I am in the Martyr's Quadrant. I've got to find a way out.

Mark brings me back in as he taps the upper-left side of the board.

"I know that was a long response to a short question, but figuring out how to get out of the Martyr's Quadrant without immediately becoming a Goldminer can be complex. If mercenaries control the company, the company easily can become a Goldminer itself. If a founder is ready to exit, becoming a Goldminer may be the best strategy. Let's talk more about this quadrant."

Mark points to the upper-left portion of the diagram. "This is the Goldminer's Quadrant. Also known as *'Show me the money!'*"

The room erupts in laughter.

"But that's what it is, right? This is the quadrant where the leader understands what it takes to be a business mercenary. This is capitalism at its most extreme—the survival of the fittest. Bottom line, Goldminers know how to make money, and they enjoy doing it.

"Leaders in this quadrant know how to make it rain through precise execution. Henry Ford also said, 'Vision without execution is hallucination.' Those in the Goldminer's Quadrant are masters at sales and strategy and implementation. They know how to squeeze blood from a turnip and then plant it again. They buy low, sell high, and do it day in and day out. These disciplines are what good venture capitalists bring to the table. They have playbooks and benchmarks for how to make money. For the Goldminer, making money is like breathing. Speaking of breathing, everybody please stand and stretch, take a breath, then sit right back down, and in five minutes we'll press on."

9

MOVING TOWARD THRIVING

"Got your breath? Good. Those in the Goldminer's Quadrant know how to swim with the sharks. They know how to compete ferociously, and they understand that if you can't fight, you'll die. Without preparing for battle well, you will not be sustainable. I love the old saying *we may stumble and fall but shall rise again; it should be enough if we did not run away from the battle.*"

> "We may stumble and fall but shall rise again; it should be enough if we did not run away from the battle." —Ghandi

---

That is me. Running from the battle. I thought about Sensors Everywhere. Because of my own lack of self-confidence and courage, we have become unsustainable without an infusion of capital. We soon will die without getting some cash or a serious breakthrough.

"For those in this quadrant, the greatest mission is to

make money. This quadrant is about operations, execution, getting rid of the non-performers, tracking the key performance indicators, and getting the systems as lean and mean as possible.

"Let me give you an example. If you dug up gold in your backyard, what would you do with it?" Everyone looks around at each other, trying to understand whether this is a trick question.

"You eventually would sell it when you believe the market for gold is high. Gold discovered in the backyard doesn't have much value other than a monetary one.

"So, what does the Goldminer have to fear?" Mark asks rhetorically.

"Well, for starters, people are made to desire more than money. When those in the Goldminer's Quadrant lose their way, it's easy for them—and everyone who works for them— to become disillusioned. When the thrill of the battle wears off, employees in a Goldminer's organization run out of passion—the fuel of life. Being a Goldminer is an exit strategy, not a sustainability strategy.

"Having a job is not a bad thing. Making good money sure isn't a bad thing. As Forrest Gump says, 'It's one less thing to worry about.' But without meaning, people implode in this quadrant. It's just not sustainable to make this quadrant your home.

"Just as there is little economic resource at the bottom of the Martyr's Quadrant, there is very little meaning at the far-left part of the Goldminer's Quadrant.

"We've all heard stories of overnight millionaires who stumbled on their fortunes with a gas station Powerball ticket. Studies have demonstrated time and time again that these people not only usually lose their fortunes, but they lose their families and friends as well. Money without purpose is a false drug, a false sense of security.

"For some of us, it's easy to criticize those in the Gold-miner's Quadrant. But it's important to keep in mind that people in this quadrant are not inherently evil—not at all. It's about security and responsibility, both incredibly important traits for those who want to take care of their families. But the Achilles' heel for the Goldminer is the absence of meaning, the absence of what gets us up in the morning and gives us the desire to make a difference in the world."

Mark pauses, walks back to the podium, and takes a drink of water. He stands for a moment without saying anything. Then, like a master storyteller, he leans forward.

"Here's the thing . . ." he says, "you can live from your heart and make a difference as a missionary. And you can make a lot of money and employ people as a mercenary. But if you can align the passion of a missionary with the execution of a mercenary, you get serious synergy.

"Because of the rapid rise of digital and exponential technologies and the connected global economy, there has never been a better time in history to be a thriving entrepreneur. In fact, I believe that for virtually every entrepreneur, and certainly every one of you here, it's possible to align your passion with a vibrant economic engine. Did you hear what I just said? Right here, right now, you have a better chance of making a living out of what you are passionate about than any other time in the history of the world. Yes, monetizing your passion. That's what we call a thriving entrepreneur.

"Time is our greatest resource in life. If you are able to use most of your time on what you are passionate about— what you were created to offer to the world—your life can produce exponential impact. In fact, given how technology has made information costs negligible, the incredible synergies we are experiencing could enable our society to move from an economy of scarcity into an economy of abundance. This is synergy on steroids. It's more than where $1 + 1 = 3$; it's where $5 + 5 = 25$. This is more than Moore's law; it's closer to Metcalfe's law regarding the exponential impact of networks.

"The exponential age brought about by digital technologies has produced companies like Google and Facebook. These companies have platforms for exponential growth. Google doesn't create all the websites; it just has a platform for organizing all the websites. Facebook doesn't write all the social media content; it just provides a platform where others provide the content. Now, imagine that your gifts have a platform that can easily find others who have a need or desire for your gifts. This could create an abundant economy.

"I know I am getting off track here, but let's reflect on the implications of this last statement—from scarcity to abundance. I know that Adam Smith might be quaking in his grave by me saying this, but this is possible through exponential technologies.

"This would be a society where almost everyone could make a living doing what they love to do. I'm not saying that making a living includes driving a Ferrari, but it does mean making a sufficient amount of money for subsistence—for sustainability—enough money to put food on the table and a roof over our heads while doing what we love to do. To me, sufficiency equals abundance.

"There are artists who have figured out how to sell their art online, singers who have been discovered on YouTube, and writers who have written *New York Times* best sellers by self-publishing on Amazon. People who love cats have made a fortune with blogs and YouTube channels. Drone enthusiasts have formed online communities that generate significant ad revenue. I could go on and on. Technology is giving the opportunity for humanity to thrive like never before. Yes, technology can be used for evil, but it also can be used for good.

"With patience and a little good direction, chances are that you can turn your hobby or passion into a legitimate business. You can experience the synergy that comes from being both a passion-driven missionary and an income-generating mercenary on the digital platform."

Mark is getting really animated. It is obvious that he is really enthusiastic about this—that he believes what he is saying. As I look over at Maya, I can see hope beaming from her face. I certainly am getting even more excited.

"I know I am getting off topic here and am going down a rabbit hole, but I do want to whet your appetite about what is happening in this new and exciting generation. Here's what I want you to hear this morning. Whatever quadrant you are in, the goal we want to challenge you with this weekend is to move toward the center, more toward the Thriver's Quadrant. Please note that you can be in the Thriver's Quadrant and still lean toward the missionary side of the quadrant. Although by definition your organization must be sustainable in this quadrant, you don't have to maximize profit and growth to live in this quadrant. For example, you might choose to make less profit and share more with your employees and your community. This choice may or may not mean that the organization makes less in the short term, but it still can make plenty to survive.

"At this retreat, we want to paint a clear picture of what it would be like to be a Thriver and then do an honest gap analysis so you can begin to take the steps necessary to move into the Thriver's Quadrant. Our goal is for everyone to live a life of exponential impact, both for yourselves and our world.

"The hard truth is that none of these three quadrants—Dreamer, Martyr, or Goldminer—is sustainable long term. They represent finite organizations. Eventually, if you don't change something, both the leaders and the employees in them implode. But by moving to the Thriver's Quadrant, you can become an infinite organization and a thriving leader. This quadrant gives you so many choices. Here you don't have to make decisions from a place of desperation."

Mark walks back across the stage.

"Any Trekkies here? Remember the Vulcan mind meld? What I'm talking about is melding the mercenary mindset with the missionary mindset. There is magic in turning your career *into* a calling. It's about purpose *and* profit, being sustainable with infinite possibilities and exponential impact."

My cell phone suddenly buzzes. I don't recognize the number, so I send an automatic message to the number saying I'll call later.

Mark continues, "I'm willing to bet most of you are either goldminers or martyrs. Actually, that's a safe bet because that's partially why you were selected to be here. The purpose of this weekend is to help you move from wherever you are closer to the Thriver's Quadrant.

"All quadrants outside of the Thriver's Quadrant are places, as Thoreau said, where you 'lead lives of quiet desperation.' No other quadrant is sustainable and truly meaningful in the long term. This is the only quadrant where you can survive the test of time doing what you love to do. This is where the two edges converge in exponential, meaningful work."

My mind feels like we've run a 10K, but Mark hardly looks winded.

"Okay, so we've discussed the four quadrants, a deeper look at the mercenary and missionary thinking. In your groups last night, you identified yourself as mostly missionary or mercenary. Today, as we've done with the quadrants, I challenge you to take that deeper. Do you have the courage to talk about not just which mindset you identify with but *why* you think you might identify more with being in a particular quadrant? I know this is asking you to reveal more about yourselves, but I promise you it will be worth it.

"You signed up for this retreat because you want to be a better leader, a *Thriver*. We could go over all the practical steps you need to get from where you are to where you want to be, and there will be a time and place for that. But as I discussed before, the first step to becoming a Thriver is *self-awareness*. You have to be willing to do a personal deep dive. So, that's what this retreat is really about—personal growth."

I sense the entire room shifting a bit uncomfortably. At least I am.

"And we're going to begin right now, in your groups."

Mark walks away as soft acoustic music begins to play. I'm not looking around, but I hear our table take a collective breath.

Once again, Jack turns to us. "Outside?" We all nod and stand and file out of the room. "Okay, as we walk, I want each of you to think about what it means to be in the quadrant you're in and maybe why you're there."

Jack leads us across a field and around a building. We end up on a trail, and as we walk, Jack suddenly becomes our nature guide, telling us about the rocks and landscape and history of the area. It is obvious he is passionate about it. He is alive and authentic. It is a refreshing change from the usual BS I am prisoner to in normal business settings. We hike for about ten minutes and end up on an outcropping of rocks, looking out over an amazing vista.

We sit for a moment, and Kyle is the first to break the silence.

"So, how do I do it?"

I turn and see Kyle standing nearby. I can see a look of frustration on his face.

"Do what?" Alex asks.

"How do I get out?"

"Out of the box?" Jack asks.

"Yes. I'm so tired of being a martyr. I don't want to kill myself, my employees, or my family. I'm tired of working my butt off for beans. I'm tired of my wife wondering if we're going to be able to pay the mortgage. I'm tired of constantly comparing myself with my friends and coming up short. I'm tired of putting on a smile for everyone around me when I feel like crap inside. I don't know. I just don't think I'm cut out for any of this."

The big guy is fuming. Right here, in front of us. And then, as quickly as it started, it stops. Kyle clears his throat and takes a deep breath.

"Let's talk about it, Kyle," Jack suggests.

"No, no, I'm fine. It's okay. I have no idea where that came from, but I'm okay. I'll be okay. Sorry, I'm cool."

"Are you sure?" Maya asks.

"Yes, I'm fine. Please, it's okay. I'm good. I didn't mean to get upset."

"But that's okay, Kyle," Jack says. "In fact, it might be exactly what you need. Get out of your comfort zone and get real. Let go. You can't just hold it in."

"Seriously," Kyle says, turning to Jack, imploring him. "I'm okay. I'm good."

We all sit for a moment.

"Boy, that session was just too close to home," Alex suddenly offers. "I definitely want to leave a legacy, but not that of a Goldminer."

"What do you mean?" Jack asks.

"The thing is, I've been at my company for ten years now. I started it from almost nothing, and I've grown it to nearly a half-billion-dollar valuation. But here's the truth . . ." She pauses for a moment as she stares at the valley below.

"I don't love it anymore. Mark is right; it is not sustainable for me."

No one speaks.

"I mean, I loved the start-up phase, the thrill of the chase. I know it sounds weird, but if there's blood in the water, I'm all in. If we're the big underdog, I'm all in. But now that we're a bigger company, I feel like I'm losing my own way.

"I don't know. It's just that lately I've felt like maybe the company would be better served by someone who is more passionate about where to take the organization. Don't get me wrong. I've been able to be incredibly hard-driving, and we've built a company that's been highly successful. I'm very proud of what we've accomplished. But I think in order to scale to the next level, I'm going to have to be someone I'm not. I don't know. I'm still processing." Alex pauses.

Her words hit me hard. She is verbalizing what I am actually going through, a situation where a leadership change is probably important to move the organization into the Thriver's Quadrant. The only difference is that Alex is stuck as a Goldminer while I'm stuck as a Martyr. But we're both stuck.

"Me too," Evan says.

I'm honestly surprised to hear him say anything at all. All day it's seemed that he's been distracted, pulling out his smartphone even though there isn't any signal and smartphones were discouraged from the start. I turn and see him sitting on a rock by himself.

"I'm trying to be a mercenary. I really am. But I feel like I'm losing myself and the people around me. I just don't know why. I think I did pretty good as a Dreamer, but now that I've got a legitimate company on my hands, I'm not so sure I know how to get everyone on the same page. And you know what? If I'm honest, I don't really want anyone's help. For some reason, I want to do it all myself."

He pauses a beat.

"That's my dragon. I'm not afraid to tell you. My dragon is my pride. Not sure how I'm going to kick it, but I know that I have to."

Again, no one says anything. I can't help but respect Evan for his honesty.

Jack speaks into the pause. "Here's the thing. Based on where each of you falls on the diagram, you all need to move. All of you. That's normal. Most people are never honest enough with themselves and self-aware enough, and consequently they never challenge themselves enough to get out of their comfort quadrants. But you all have what it takes to make the move."

"I'm just not sure how to do that," Maya says. "I think as an artist I've always viewed people who made money, capitalists or whatever you want to call them, as inherently greedy, bad people. I thought about it as either/or. Capitalist or compassionate, money or mission. But I see now that I'm wrong.

"Honestly," Maya says, looking at Alex, "I love the way that you are so confident and that you're a woman crushing it in business. It's obvious that you're not intimidated by anyone. And I know what you said, but I sense that you aren't just in it for the money." If I could bring your strengths to how I do things, I could do so much more for others and for my art."

"To be honest," Maya continued, "I wish I had more of what you do. If I could bring your strengths to how I do things, I could do so much more for others and for my art. I was sort of shocked to see my name anywhere outside of the Dreamer's quadrant." She turned to Jack with a questioning look.

"I think you are both very strong and capable people," Jack said.

We all nodded in agreement.

"Alex, your vulnerability is as much a show of strength as anything else you've said or done. And Maya, you are definitely beyond the Dreamer's Quadrant. You have all the components of a going concern. To be sure, you're more squarely in the Martyr's Quadrant than you are in the Gold-miner's Quadrant, but at least you are out of the gate. Now, you just need to figure out how to turn the dial so that you can thrive. That's why this moment is such an important part of your journey."

"Huh. I never thought of it like that. Well, I sure hope so." Maya smiles slightly. "Thanks."

I have to admit, I wasn't prepared for this level of vulnerability. Not that it's bad—because it's not. It's so good and refreshing. I just wasn't prepared for it.

"Let's take a break for a bit now," Jack says, "and then we'll all meet in front of the cookhouse after lunch for our afternoon session. Try to take some time alone between now and then. Remember, this retreat is all about awareness—first of ourselves, then of others on our team, and finally of the community and world around us. What happened last night and just now is all about awareness. It's not until we are truly honest with ourselves that genuine change can happen.

Awareness is the magic sword that can slay the dragons. Okay, see you all back after lunch."

WE HAVE AN HOUR BEFORE LUNCH. As we all walk back down the trail, I notice that Jack is lingering behind by himself. It is a bit of a rare moment to find Jack alone, so I stay back until I'm closer to him.

"Jack?"

"Hey, Chad, what's on your mind?"

"Do you have any plans during the break? I know we're supposed to go the solitude route, but honestly I just need to process a bit."

"Sure. I'd love to," Jack says, to my surprise. "There's a great path not far from here that winds down along the stream. Let's go."

As we start down the trail, Jack says, "So, tell me what you're thinking."

I take a long breath.

"Well, there's no question that I'm motivated by the missionary mindset. Things like vision and purpose and mission come naturally to me. But I'm also beginning to see clearly that I live, and thereby my organization lives, in the Martyr's Quadrant. I hate even saying that.

"I'm great at getting people to jump on board with my vision, but I'm not any good at driving the needed execution of our organization. And the truth is, I'm stuck. Honestly, I just can't keep going on like this."

"I get it," Jack says. "Sounds to me like this is a matter of you becoming more comfortable in the mercenary mindset. And more than that, I think it's about you being comfortable with yourself and willing to be who you're afraid to be."

I stop on the trail. "What do you mean?"

"Listen, Chad. I don't know what happened in your past, but someone or something told you that you couldn't make it, that you didn't have what it takes."

He pauses a beat. "And you believed it."

I can feel the blood flushing my face. No, I'm not going to allow myself to go there. At least not yet.

"Let's just say that I've seen my share of people lead through fear and intimidation," I say, "and I guess I made a vow back then never to lead that way."

"Vows can be beautiful, Chad," Jack responds without a hint of judgment. "They can also be deadly. You know that in order for you to become all that you can be, you're going to have to pick up that sword and fight again. For your family. For your company. For yourself."

"I know, but I'm simply not that guy. Besides, I just don't know how to do that without leaving carnage in my wake. I don't want to be the kind of organization where the leader walks all over everyone and fires good people to accomplish what he wants—to make money. I'm not willing to do that. If that means I lose my company, then so be it."

Now the conversation is getting under my skin. As much as everyone admires this guy, he doesn't know me. He doesn't know my real story or my real pain or the constant accusations in my head. I sure don't need another accuser now. If he wants to accuse me, he can stand in line behind all the accusers in my head. And I'm not ready to open it up. We are done.

"Look, Jack," I say, "I appreciate you taking time with me like this. I really do. But I'm not looking for some psychological counseling session. I need real answers to my very real problems. I'm sorry I'm not the guy you think I am. I'm not that person. I'm not a mercenary."

I pause again.

"I'm a martyr. And that might be all I'll ever be."

"Well, Chad, I'm sorry, but I simply don't believe that. Anyway, it's worth at least trying while you're here. It's worth trying to get your mercenary strength back. And that voice inside you that is dogging you, it's just not speaking the truth."

Jack smiles warmly. "Okay, I've gotta run. I'll see you after lunch."

AFTER JACK LEAVES, I realize that I am seething inside. This retreat is nothing like I thought it would be. I was expecting to learn tips and techniques and strategies to enhance my leadership and grow my business. I wasn't prepared for it to get this personal. I didn't sign up for this. I sit on a nearby bench to gather my thoughts.

Suddenly, I remember that I missed a call earlier during the session. I walk back to the cookhouse because it is the only place at the ranch with Internet service. I pull out my phone and send a text back to the number that called me.

ME: This is Chad Banning. Sorry I missed a call earlier.

UNKNOWN: Hi, Mr. Banning, this is Cameron, from InvestCorp.

ME: Oh, hi. What's up?

CAMERON: I was texting to see if I could get a number for your partner. I must have misplaced his business card.

ME: My partner? What do you mean?

CAMERON: He said his name was Eric, that he works with you.

ME: When did you see Eric?

CAMERON: Today. He and Marcus met for quite a

while, but there were two things Marcus forgot to mention. I just need to relay those before the end of the day. I'm sorry. I guess I figured you knew about the meeting.

(Long pause)

ME: Well, that's good to know. Thank you for the heads up. I'll text you Eric's contact info.

CAMERON: Thank you very much.

I'm stunned. Why would Eric be meeting with Marcus? Then it hits me. He's trying to go behind my back and put the deal together. After all, he did say that he thought it was the best thing for the company.

He's trying to push me out.

10

A SUDDEN SHIFT

The next morning, I wake early. Given that I have plenty of time, I decide to try a little mindfulness. If there is science behind a technique to calm the fear-invoking chatter of my mind, that dragon inside me, I want to give it a try. I am able to do it for five minutes, which is a record for me.

After a quick breakfast with our team, Jack gives us instructions to get changed into clothes that we don't mind getting wet and then to meet again at the big parking lot.

Waiting for us in the parking lot are three old yellow school buses. Tied to the top of each are bright yellow rafts that read *River Raiders* on the side.

"Well, this should be fun," Alex says sarcastically as we walk toward the buses.

"Come on, Alex," Evan says. "This will be awesome! After all, you're the Barbarian."

"You're telling me you're totally cool with this?" Kyle says to Evan.

"Well, truth be told, I worked for a summer as a rafting guide on the Ocoee River in Tennessee. Trust me, I don't like to be out of control. Thankfully, in this case, I won't be." With that, Evan runs past us and jumps on one of the buses.

"Does that guy drive anyone else crazy?" Kyle asks. "I mean, what *hasn't* he done?"

"Well, these guys might think they're the River Raiders," Alex says, "but I like to keep my raiding to the boardroom."

We all laugh.

As I look at the buses, I can't help but think of the bus Chris McCandless died alone in, the one featured on the cover of Krakauer's *Into the Wild*. I recall a line from his journal: "Happiness [is] only real when shared." As I look around at my group, I sense such happiness to be doing whatever it is we're about to do with them, instead of doing it alone. I've definitely been challenged this weekend to step into more mercenary thinking. But I'm also beginning to wonder if it's even possible to do this alone.

As soon as we're all seated on board the bus, Jack stands and tells us what most of us already figured out. "Well, there's no hiding the fact that we're going to do a bit of white-water rafting today. So, who's been rafting before?"

Evan and I raise our hands. That leaves Alex, Kyle, and Maya as the newbies. None of them is excited.

"Don't worry, this is one of the best rafting outfits in Colorado. They're experts and will take all the time we need to make sure we're well-trained and prepared for the water."

"Jack, what class of river are we doing today?" Evan probes.

"Classes III and IV. There's one small section that may be a V."

"Is that good?" Alex asks.

"Depends on what you mean by good," Evan laughs. "There are only six classes of rivers, so you'd better buckle up. Class VI is basically a death wish."

Jack smiles. "Well, there's definitely some risk involved, but as long as we work as a team and follow instructions, we should be totally fine."

Somehow Evan convinces the rafting company to allow him to guide us on the river. Even though it is clear Evan knows what he is doing on the water, I can tell this isn't much consolation for Alex, Kyle, or Maya.

It takes us an hour or so to get to the drop-off point. Once there, we help get the rafts off the bus, stand through a long and very thorough safety and instructional session, then don wet suits and walk to the water's edge.

One by one, we step into the boat. I look around. Here we are, a group of eclectic entrepreneurs, along with our trusty leader, and a brave and very arrogant guide. Before we know it, we're heading downstream.

Alex is sitting next to me. I can see she is literally white-knuckling the paddle in her hands. She's wearing sunglasses, but I have a hunch that under the dark lenses are eyes intensely focused on the river ahead. And her body language is speaking loud and clear: "I'm not taking any chances with my life."

For the first hour or so, we spend most of the time gawking at the scenery. A perfect Colorado breeze of sage and mountains fills the air. Red-rocked canyons tower above us, cut out of the rock by centuries of water flowing from the jagged peaks of the Rockies on its way to the Pacific Ocean. Bright yellow aspens flank the river, and we watch as a pair of eagles circles above us. Is this a dream?

Ahead of us, we can see that there are small rapids, probably Class II or III at the most.

"What do we do?" Maya asks.

"Nothing. Just enjoy the view. I've got this," Evan says.

"What?" Kyle says. "I thought we all needed to work

together to successfully make it down the river. That's what the guy said back in the information session."

"Yeah, well, they say that because they want you to be part of the ride. If these were Class IV rapids, then yes, we'd need the strength of the team. But I can handle this. You guys just enjoy yourselves."

As we enter the white water, Evan deftly maneuvers us through the small rapids. Even Alex and Maya seem to ease up a bit. Before I know it, we're all laughing and having a great time together. But that doesn't last long.

Some people believe things don't happen suddenly. I've always thought such people to be incredibly naive. Life can change on a dime. In an instant, what has been a beautifully flowing river transforms into a menacing tumble of white water.

The canyon walls have narrowed so much that the river is pushing more water through a much smaller gap. The raft is being tossed around like a cork in a storm.

"Hang on, everyone. I've got this!" Evan yells.

That's when I see it. I know that Evan couldn't have seen it because of the angle of the boat. A tree branch is sticking out into the river, hanging precariously over the water. For a moment, everything seems to move in slow motion.

"Evan!"

But it's too late. Just as Evan turns around, the branch smashes into his head, easily knocking him off the raft. I look over the edge of the raft, and I can see Evan. He is floating facedown in the water, moving quickly along with the current.

What happens next shocks all of us.

Big Kyle stands up, unhooks his feet from the raft, and jumps over the edge of the boat. We all watch as he tumbles around in the water until he is side by side with Evan. He snatches Evan up and spins him around. Lying on his back, Kyle kicks and swims with Evan, following the boat.

"Paddle forward!" someone yells.

I look back. It's Maya. She had been sitting next to Evan and is now sitting in his seat.

We all dig our paddles into the water as hard as we can. The boat barely misses a rock on the right side. My heart is pumping. I glance over at Alex. I am surprised. Instead of looking frightened, she looks steely eyed and focused. Her jaw is set, like a soldier waiting for the next command.

Suddenly, I realize that we're stuck on a rock. And the middle of the raft is beginning to buckle.

"Over right!" Maya shouts. I remember the command means that those on the right side are supposed to dig in and everyone else is supposed to lean in toward the right to balance out the boat.

I am on the left side, so I lunge toward my right, next to Alex.

"Hold on!" Maya yells.

I grab the rope that circles the bottom of the boat and hold on for dear life.

"Get down!" Jack shouts. "Hold on and get down!"

Everyone ducks into the boat, which is now beginning to fill with water. We are leaning hard to the right, and I am sure the boat is about to pop up and tip over under all the pressure.

And then it happens. One end of the boat lifts and the other end flips over, dumping us all out of the boat and into the water.

For a moment, I am totally disoriented. I struggle to find the surface of the water. I panic. My head bangs against a rock, and the sound echoes in my helmet. I struggle for breath. Then, as if on cue, I pop out of the water—thank

God for life jackets! I tuck my knees to my chest as they taught us. The worst of it is over. I look around and see Evan and Kyle and the others. Everyone, that is, except for Alex.

Then I spot her. She is clinging to the raft, still hanging on to the rope that is attached around the edge of the raft.

"Let go!" Jack yells.

Alex looks terrified. "I . . . I can't!"

"Yes, you can. Just let go and float feet-first in the current. You'll be fine. We've got you!"

I watch as a very non-barbarian-looking Alex finally lets go of the raft. For a moment, she seems to struggle in the water, but then she heads toward the milder eddy just like the rest of us.

The boat, along with our drenched group, finally comes to the end of the white water and slows as it enters a stretch of calm water. We all swim to the shore and sit there, coughing, heaving breaths, and exchanging dead stares. Evan and Kyle are already on the shore. They seem okay.

No one speaks for a moment.

"WELL, I think that's the worst of it," Jack says, breaking the silence.

Suddenly we all erupt with cheers and high fives and even a few tears, though the water hides them perfectly. We survived—together.

A few minutes later Jack begins unpacking a well-deserved riverside meal. We are all glad the boat was recovered and that the food was kept safe in a compartment in the raft. Even though we're grateful to be alive, everyone is silent. So much has happened in such a short period of time. We are exhausted but grateful.

Evan speaks first.

"I . . . I don't know what to say," he blurts out.

"Dude, you did what you . . ." Kyle starts. Evan cuts him off.

"No, I was acting like an idiot. I thought I could control the situation. I acted like I didn't need you guys."

He turns to us.

"I'm so sorry. I don't know why I do that. I don't know why I've struggled so much to work with others. That was a horrible display of arrogance."

"It's okay," Jack says. "Your team needs you. You're better with a team, Evan. You have to know that. You are so capable and talented, but it's only once you start trusting your team, serving your team, that you'll really step into your sweet spot."

"Your Thriver's Quadrant," Maya says.

"I'd like that," Evan says with a small smile. "In the spirit of that, how about Kyle? I didn't know he was David Hassel-hoff in disguise. Dude, that was like a big-time *Baywatch* move."

We all laugh.

"I don't know," Kyle says. "Something just took over in me. Honestly, I think it's been building for the past few days. To tell you the truth, the word I put into the fire on the first night was *shame*."

"Shame?" Jack asks.

"I think I've lived my entire professional life in shame of being a martyr, although until this retreat I've never used that word to describe it. I've watched good people get fired, bills go unpaid to vendors, and even my family's disappointment that I wasn't living to my full potential."

He pauses for a moment, gathering his thoughts and emotions.

"I was worried that if I was successful in business, my parents would think I was a sellout. Because they lived as missionaries for so long, I thought they would think less of me if I did anything less than that. But now I know that's the opposite of the truth.

"I've allowed other people's opinions to hold me captive to the point that I've been immobilized. When Evan fell over the edge, I just knew that I needed to act, not think about it or ponder the risk but simply act."

"Dude . . . I'm so glad you did. Literally, the missionary saved the mercenary's life!" Evan said.

"Alex, do you want to talk about what happened back there?" Jack asks, once again shaping the conversation.

Alex is staring at the river.

"I couldn't let go," she says. "I don't know why, but I just couldn't let go."

"It's okay," Maya says. "That was scary. We all felt it."

"Thanks, Maya, but it's more than that," Alex says. "I've never been able to let go. I don't know why, but I've always held on to things and tried to stay in control out of fear."

Everyone is still as Alex continues.

"Honestly, I think it goes all the way back to when I was a kid. I think I'm just afraid of failure. That's what I wrote down and threw into the fire. Do you know why my name is Alex?"

No one says anything, but we can all see Alex's tears.

"It's because my dad wanted a boy so badly that even when he knew he was having a girl, he gave me a name that would remind him of the boy he never had."

It's clear Alex is struggling to keep it together, but right now that doesn't matter.

"I've spent my entire life trying to be the man that my dad wanted me to be. I did whatever it took. Failure has never been an option. But all I ever really wanted was his approval. I know, cliché-ridden daddy issues. But they're real for me. And here's the weird thing—for the first time in my life, I feel like I've got it; he accepts me for who I am and for not what I do."

"And you don't want to let go?" Jack asks.

"No, I don't," Alex says. "I've sacrificed everything to get here. But now, somehow, I realize that for me to overcome my shadow self, I have to slay the dragon of self-reliance and fear of failure, and I've got to reach out to others to help me find my way."

She stands up.

"I've lost my way. I know it. I just don't know how to find meaning again. I know that somehow I have to, but I just can't figure it out. Regardless, this is the start. I can't stay this way."

"Me too," Maya says. Everyone turns to her.

"Thank you, Alex," Maya says with a smile on her face but with tears in her eyes. "Watching you and listening to you, I know what I need to do."

"What?" Alex asks.

"My mother used to tell me that I need to stop living the pain of my past or worrying about my future, but learn to live in the present. She was right. And I think I know the first thing I need to do. I need to call my father and tell him the truth. I'm finished with posing. It's time to be the authentic me."

11

STRENGTHS AND SHADOWS

The events of the afternoon have left our group more than a little rattled—and changed. Even as our bus drives back into camp and drops us off, everyone in our group seems different. We have crossed some sort of threshold. Everyone, that is, except me. As much as I loved seeing the transformation in each of the others, I am anxious for something more.

During dinner Maya tells us about the phone call with her dad. She recounts how quickly her father forgave her and how he said that he was proud of her no matter what. A massive weight is off Maya's shoulders, and now she says, "I just needed to start wielding my sword along with my paintbrush."

After dinner, we all meet back together for our final evening session.

Not long after we arrive, Mark is back on stage, recounting the events of the day. Team leaders take turns giving recaps. Every team there, it seems, experienced their own adventures and faced their own dragons. One team talks about a harrowing day rock climbing and rappelling. Another one talks about a ropes course that had been both maddening and freeing. And, of course, Jack talks about our near-death experience on the river.

When the teams have each reported back, Mark gives his final talk of the weekend. He opens with a series of film clips, ending on a montage of scenes about Aragorn from *The Lord of the Rings*. Mark talks about Aragorn's journey and how his name changed along with it. In the beginning of the movie, Aragorn is known as Strider or simply as "the Ranger." Even though Aragorn was born as an heir to the throne, it took facing his shadow self, finding his fellowship, and accepting his true name before he could step into his destiny.

"The truth is," Mark says, "each of you has incredible potential to be a Thriver. But to be who you were born to be, you must be willing to be aware of yourself—your strengths and your shadows. You must be willing to bring others along with you on your journey; you simply cannot be your best self without authentic fellowship around you. And finally, you must be willing to understand the greater role you play in the world, accept who you really are, and step into your destiny."

Even as Mark is speaking, I can feel something stirring inside of me. He is right. I know that I need to make some big changes. There is still more for me to accomplish at Sensors Everywhere, but I sense that I have to somehow see myself differently and no longer listen to my negative chatter. I just don't know how to do that.

"I want to thank you all for being willing to go *below the waterline* and be authentic with each other. I'm reminded of a saying that *the lack of transparency results in distrust and a deep sense of insecurity. But, with the realization of one's own potential and self confidence in one's ability, one can build a better world.*"

"The lack of transparency results in distrust and a deep sense of insecurity… but, with the realization of one's own potential and self confidence in one's ability, one can build a better world."—Dalai Lama

As MARK NEARS the end of his talk, he reaches down and picks up a small wooden box. He opens it.

"I hope that you all really understand the importance of being fully aware as the first step to being fully alive. I know that we've talked a lot about identity tonight. I know that so many of us have lived our entire lives listening to the wrong voices. Sometimes the voices come from loved ones but leave unintentional wounds; sometimes the voices come from society around us; and sometimes the voices come from within, from our own personal critic."

That is me.

"And even though I think we realize that we must stop listening to the wrong voices, it's sometimes hard to know which voices are the right ones. That's partly why we started the Entrepreneur's Retreat. We wanted there to be a safe place where leaders could take an honest personal inventory, face their dragons, and learn the joy and synergy of being a Thriver.

"In this box, I have a symbol of everything we've talked about this weekend." Mark reaches into the small box and retrieves what appears to be a silver ring.

"This is what we call the *Thriver's Signet*. It's a simple ring, engraved with a very important icon—an infinity symbol. The infinity symbol represents the infinite and exponential potential of a Thriver. As you might recall, the only quadrant that is sustainable and that can survive the test of time—or in other words, be infinite—is the Thriver's Quadrant. The other three are finite. One of the traditions we have here at Six Peaks is the practice of giving these rings to others and at the same time telling the receiver of the ring what we've seen in them as a Thriver. These rings can't be bought for oneself but only given to another, because true and healthy glory is not taken—it is recognized by others and then bestowed.

"Another of the great joys of this retreat," Mark adds, "is working with some really amazing team facilitators. Tonight, one of our facilitators, Jack Angel, has asked to publicly give away a Thriver's Signet."

Jack stands and moves to the podium. Mark hands him the small wooden box.

"This weekend, our team has been through a lot," he says. "We've faced some fierce dragons. We've gotten to know each other in amazing ways. Truthfully, I'd love to give a ring to each member of our team, but there are a couple people who I want to acknowledge publicly."

He pauses a beat.

"Kyle, would you come join me up here?" I turn to see Kyle's face suddenly flush. He stands up and walks to the front.

"Kyle, I've loved learning your story, and I've been honored to be part of it this weekend." Jack turns to us in the audience. "Kyle's parents are amazing people, literal missionaries in Central America. Kyle has had an amazing deposit of both missionary and mercenary since he was young. He's both compassionate and passionate, humble and strong."

Jack turns back to Kyle.

"I know that you've felt conflicted stepping into the mercenary role in your life. I know that you've faced shame as a martyr. But today, I want you to know that we see in you an amazingly vision-driven missionary but also a decisive, powerful mercenary. Listen, Kyle. You are not timid. You are not less than. You are a leader. You are bold. We all watched you jump into a raging river, not hesitating for a second, to save a friend. That's who you are—decisive, bold, strategic, and smart. Today, I give you this ring as your friend. This is a symbol of who you are, who you really are. Not a monk, but a Thriver. You have what it takes. Let this ring serve as a monument, an eternal reminder of the words of truth spoken to you today."

Tears well from Kyle's eyes. It is obvious Jack is hitting a nerve with him, with all of us."

"You know," Kyle adds, "one of my favorite philosophers once said *life must be understood backward, but that it must be lived forward*. I'm not sure I ever really believed that. But I do now. I can see how my backstory is playing such an important part in my bigger story. Needless to say, the past is all beginning to make more sense to me." He turned to Jack.

"Thank you for believing in me. You and our small cohort all pulled for me this week. I could feel it and I needed it. Thank you!"

"Life must be understood backward. But it must be lived forward." – Søren Kierkegaard

---

It is an amazing moment. And though I am thrilled for Kyle, as he walks back to our table, I have to admit that I am a bit jealous.

"I'd also like to call Maya to the stage," Jack says.

I turn to see Maya, eyes wide with surprise. We all cheer and applaud as she stands up and makes her way to the stage. Jack stands next to her, towering over her small frame.

"Okay, so I just told you all about how Kyle literally risked his life to help rescue one of our team members. But what I didn't tell you is that the team member who needed rescuing was also our fearless rafting guide. That means when our guide fell from the boat, we were captain-less."

For a moment, I am reliving the events in my mind. It really had been a harrowing experience.

"But," Jack continues, "that moment was short-lived. A moment after our guide fell from the boat, Maya jumped into the guide's place and fearlessly took the helm of the boat, even though she had never rafted before! She stepped up with total poise and confidence. She was a vivid picture of grace under pressure . . . her mercenary and missionary traits both working in concert. She also had the courage after the rafting trip to call her dad and have a difficult but redeeming conversation."

He turns to Maya.

"Maya, you are an amazing artist. But you are so much more than just an artist. You are an artist with a pretty intense dose of warrior mixed in. In fact, today you reminded me of Wonder Woman."

We all laugh.

"But I really mean that. That character is supposed to be a personification of feminine power, a perfect image of what it means to be a Thriver, able to wield the sword and live from your heart at the same time. And as we have talked about so much this weekend, when you can do that, you create exponential impact in your life, in your organization, and with your legacy."

Jack reaches into the box and pulls out another ring. This one is more elegant than the one he'd given to Kyle.

"Maya, you demonstrated undaunted courage and amazing leadership today. I'm honored to give you this

Thriver's Signet as a reminder of the incredible step you took today. Never again see yourself as a starving artist. You are not a starving artist. You are a creative force of nature. An entrepreneur to be reckoned with."

After Maya sits down, a few other leaders take the stage and speak words over members of their teams, and a few other rings are bestowed. It is a deeply moving, almost spiritual, experience. No, not almost—it is a spiritual experience. I am watching what feels like adult rites of passage.

~

AFTER THE MEETING IS OVER, there is a big bonfire where everyone gathers for drinks as an end-to-the-weekend celebration. As I look into the fire, my mind shoots back to the first night and the folded paper that I threw in.

Next to me, Maya and Alex stand together, laughing and talking. No doubt, this weekend has created new friendships that will last a lifetime. As I stand there, I can't help but overhear the two women talking next to me.

"Okay, Alex, I'm going to step out on a limb here," Maya says.

"What?" Alex replies. "What do you mean?"

"Well, I've been thinking. I came to this retreat determined to find out what was missing in my leadership so I could somehow untangle the knot of my art and business."

"So, do you think that happened?" Alex asks.

"Well, as you know, this weekend has been less about the nuts and bolts of leadership strategy and disciplines and much more about our own personal journeys."

"Sounds like that thing with your dad was a pretty big deal," Alex says.

"For sure," Maya replies. "Just talking to him and telling

him the truth was so freeing. I've lived too much of my life trying to please other people, afraid of what others would think."

"Well, we sure as heck can't do that any more," Alex says. "I also am tired of being so afraid to fail. I've been trying to control everyone and everything around me, afraid to let go. We all know how that turns out. I'm done trying to do it all on my own."

"That's the thing," Maya says. I am sure I can hear a bit of hesitation in her voice.

"What?" Alex says.

"Well, I've been thinking about you and your desire for purpose and vision for the Barbarian Group."

Alex turns to Maya. "I'm listening."

"Alex, you are one of the most capable persons, male or female, I have ever been around. I admire your grit and determination and fearless approach to business. You are the definition of a badass woman in business."

Maya exhales. "But I think you're missing something."

There's a pause. I can see Alex's eyes narrow just slightly. "What are you saying, Maya?"

"I'm just saying that you need someone who can stand by your side and fight for the creative vision on your team. You need someone who understands innovation and creativity and story. Alex, I would like to help you make the Barbarian Group as mission-focused as it is battle-focused."

Alex is intrigued. She is smiling slightly. "Oh really? And how are you supposed to do that?"

"Honestly, I'm not entirely sure yet," Maya says. "But I have a few ideas. My projects all benefit and empower women around the world. Your company is a picture of powerful women winning. Together, I know that we can help each other."

Another pause.

"Alex, let's work together. I don't pretend to know exactly what that looks like yet, but I sense that we can bring out the best in each other. Let me bring a missionary heart to your work, and I need you to bring out the mercenary warrior in me."

An uncomfortable moment passes.

"Don't get me wrong," Maya says. "I'm not asking for a handout. But I think we can do some amazing things as a team."

Alex smiles. "Maya, I'd love that. From the first time that you spoke in the circle, I felt a connection to you and your work. I need someone like you on our team—to help us shape our culture and help us frame a story with more impact. Honestly, I think you are a missing link in our story as a company. Together, we can help hurting women around the world. I think adding a social impact component to the Barbarian Group will be a game changer."

Alex looked more genuinely excited than I'd seen her the entire week.

"I could even see myself staying at the company forever —or for at least as long as it has meaning, which is what you'd bring. You know where to find and how to help these women in need. You also are amazing at telling their stories through your art. And I have the financial resources. After all, I think it was your namesake, Maya Angelou, who said, *When we give cheerfully and accept gratefully, everyone is blessed.* So, let's do it!"

"When we give cheerfully and accept gratefully, everyone is blessed." —Maya Angelou

---

"We are going to crush it!" Maya responds. They embrace for a moment.

Wow. I am literally watching it happen in front of me. The power of the missionary and mercenary coming together, both in a person and between people, is inspiring. I am witnessing the power of synergy, of the birth of exponential impact. Although I am excited for them, I still feel a little jealous that my story will be lost during this retreat. Time is running out.

Suddenly . . . "Hey, Chad," a voice says. I feel a hand on my shoulder and turn around. It is Jack.

"I am wondering if you'd be willing to take a short hike with me. I want to show you something."

"Uh, sure," I say. And the two of us head out into the darkness.

12

CHOOSE TO BE A HERO

J ack guides me to a trail that I haven't been on yet. We slowly meander our way up the mountain. Clouds are moving across a silver moon, creating white highlights and shadows as we walk.

"You know, Chad, I really believe you were meant to be here this week. There is a positive flow to this weekend that is undeniable. Do you remember the first night I talked about the Entrepreneur's Journey?"

"Uh, yeah. You said it was a lot like the Hero's Journey."

"That's right. The first step of the Hero's Journey is the ordinary world. That's where you were before this retreat."

"What do you mean by *ordinary*?"

"I don't mean ordinary in a disparaging way at all. I simply mean that up until this weekend, you were simply living life *as you knew it*. Like Peter Parker before he knew that he was special. Or Frodo before he left the safety of the Shire. It was ordinary . . . and safe."

"Well, I might argue that my life before this retreat was

safe. Jack, all this time I've been trying to tell you that I'm about to lose Sensors Everywhere."

Jack stops.

"What do you mean?" he asks.

"Well, it's a long story, but just last week I was in a board-room with a group of venture capitalists who want to give us money in exchange for them taking control of the company and me surrendering my job."

"How did you respond?"

"I haven't given them an answer yet. But I'm not sure I have any other choice. Our company needs the money, and the truth is, my wife and I have been struggling financially at home. I also have a son who is getting ready to go to college. My wife is tired of the constant stress of the finances, and so am I. And all of this stress has made me personally distant from her and the kids."

"Listen to me, Chad. You always have a choice. Recall the journey of becoming a Thriver. Yes, you have clearly been in the Martyr's Quadrant, but there is more than one way for you to become a Thriver. For example, you can go home tomorrow and begin reducing your company's expenses and trim the fat. That would give the company a longer fuse to figure out some next steps. The term *conservative entrepreneur* is not an oxymoron.

"We all have that choice personally, too. What car we drive, what house we live in, what schools we choose for our children, where we go on our vacations. It may not seem like we have a choice sometimes, but we usually do. If you love your current job and you don't want to lose control of the company, you can choose to live within your means, both with the company and at home. And that choice often gives us the opportunity to thrive. It also gives you leverage in negotiation, when you have the option to walk out of the room without a deal."

"Jack, I'm also having to deal with Eric. He's my partner. You could say he's the detailed brain of the operation. Anyway, in the beginning, Eric and I worked well as a team, and Sensors Everywhere began to grow. We were starting to scale, and then something happened. I don't know what, but something happened and we just stopped growing. And lately, I've been feeling like Eric just wants to sell out and walk away. And sure enough, on this trip I found out that while I've been gone, he met with the VCs, trying to push an investment round and almost certainly a big-time demotion for me."

"Come on, Chad, let's keep walking. I want you to see something. We've got a bit farther to go."

As we walk, I can feel the air getting thinner. The path we are on is winding steeply uphill, and my Midwest lungs can barely keep up. But as I ponder Jack's suggestion that I really do have a choice, deep down I begin to feel some hope. Not a lot, but some.

Just then, we walk through a small stand of trees and out into a wide-open area. There are no more trees, only rock and air and sky. We are above the tree line. The sky seems to go on forever. Above me, I see stars, brighter and more of them than I've ever seen before. For a moment, neither of us says anything. I am in awe, just taking it in. A few clouds move hauntingly across the moon, painting a shimmering kaleidoscope of shapes on the rock. The whole scene is stunning. Jack leads me farther up.

"This is what the Entrepreneur's Journey is like," Jack says. "Down below, you probably had no idea what was in store for you. You had to make a choice to step into this story, and on the way it was both beautiful and painful. One moment we were smelling sage, and the next we were gasping for air. One moment we were nearly slipping on the rocks, and the next moment we are gazing at this slice of the Milky Way."

"Boy, I've felt like that in business," I say. "But lately I've just felt the storms of life. It's been so hard for me to see past my own doubts and fears. What's the next step in the Hero's Journey?"

"It's known as the *refusal of the call*."

"Ha! I did that as soon as my wife told me she'd signed me up. Tried to find every excuse in the book not to come."

"Yes, that's part of it for sure. And then you resisted again at the fire on the first night."

"How do you know I resisted at the fire?" I ask. He is right, but I never said that to him or anyone else.

"Because we always resist when we're forced to look our dragons in the face," Jack says. "It's human nature to want to turn and run. Our fight or flight or freeze instinct kicks in. But in the end, when you tossed that sheet of paper into the fire, you made your choice to cross the threshold, to embrace the call."

"Yeah, I suppose so," I say. I hadn't really thought about it, but it was true. When I threw that paper into the fire, somehow I knew I was declaring war on my inner critic, determined to do whatever it takes to become a Thriver.

"I think I remember the next step being something about allies, enemies, and tests."

"That's great," Jack nods.

"As far as my enemy, my greatest dragon, I think that's gotten much clearer, too . . ."

Just then, a massive bolt of lightning flashes across the sky. Thunder crashes almost immediately following. I've heard that the weather can change on a dime in Colorado, but this is nuts. The hair on my arms literally stands up on end. I'm almost sure I can taste metal in my mouth, like I'm chewing on that dime.

"Quick! Follow me!" Jack says, urging me just a bit farther up the path. "We're almost there."

Just then, I feel rain falling on my head. I suddenly remember all that I've heard about lightning. I also remember being rained on before the investor meeting. In this moment, I know that we are especially vulnerable. We are above the tree line, and the storm is right over our heads. But something in me feels different this time. There is a subtle peace just knowing that Jack is here.

Jack leads me up the path and turns a quick corner, and a moment later we are standing just inside the opening of a cave in the side of the mountain. And not a moment too soon. The clouds above us open, and rain begins to fall in sheets outside.

"Wow, that was close," I say.

Jack laughs. "I love it. So close to nature that we really feel alive!"

"Well, I feel alive, that's for sure!"

As my eyes adjust to the dark, I can see that the cave has been visited frequently. There is a pile of wood against one of the walls, a few wooden crates, and a dozen or so cut log stools rung around a fire pit.

"Jack, what is this place?"

"Our leadership team comes up here after every camp for debriefing. We keep wood up here and usually bring along a few cigars and nice bottles of scotch," Jack says as he works to build a fire, lighting what looks like a small bird's nest until it blooms into flames. He deftly adds wood until there's a perfect little fire burning in the cave.

"The view from here is so wide open," I say.

"I love looking at the valley. At sunset, it's even more stunning," Jack says as we sit down opposite each other. We sit quietly for a moment, listening to the rain outside. I find myself focusing on and listening to my own breathing. Wow. The ethos of this retreat really is getting to me.

"So what does it say?" Jack asks.

"What?"

"The dragon. Your enemy. Your inner critic. What does it tell you?"

I stop. I can feel my blood rising as I think about it. It is almost as though I can sense the dragon, my inner critic, right here in the cave with us.

"That I can't make it. That I don't have what it takes. That I'm just a fake, a phony, a poser—both at work and at home. That I'm going to make some major error and screw up everything I've worked for, everything so many good people have worked for. Bottom line is that I'm a failure. And that soon, everyone else will know it too. I bounce around feeling condemnation and fear about my company, my family, my marriage, my finances, my health. The list goes on and on."

I sit there, the words echoing in my head.

"Without a doubt, my inner critic is my greatest enemy, my biggest dragon. But something Mark said has really stuck with me—that I need to train my brain to watch my thoughts rather than immediately identifying with and embracing those thoughts. I've never heard that before, but it makes sense. I think mindfulness will be one of the weapons I use to fight this dragon."

"I'm so proud of how far you have come and the truths you are beginning to acknowledge," Jack responds. "You have always had what it takes within you to defeat the dragon, but it takes commitment and practice over a period of time."

"I'm ready to fight this. If I'm honest, I've fought with my inner critic my whole life. One day I'm doing okay, and the next day I'll feel like a failure and I spiral downward. I'm all over the map. But I have hope now that I don't always have to live this way."

Suddenly, Jack stands. His figure is somehow bigger and more ominous in the cave. The fire casts a shadow of his figure on the side of the cave. He is, in this moment, larger than life. He walks around the fire and stands right next to me and then reaches into his pocket.

"Chad, stand up," he says. "It's time to put a stake in the ground."

I stand as he opens a box and pulls out a Thriver's Signet.

"Chad, I don't know if you realize this, but your name actually means *warrior*. I looked it up. I see that warrior in you. I don't know what others have told you or all that your dragon has said to you, but I believe that I've been sent here this weekend to tell you that you are good enough, you are strong enough, and you have what it takes to overcome your dragon. G. K. Chesterton once said, 'Fairy tales are more than true; not because they tell us dragons exist, but because they tell us dragons can be beaten.' You are a warrior who will slay your dragon."

"Fairy tales are more than true; not because they tell us dragons exist, but because they tell us dragons can be beaten." —GK Chesterton

---

Jack reaches out and hands me the ring.

"Now, accept your true name, your true identity. Begin to slay your dragon. You can walk out of this cave a new man.

In all the best ways, both a missionary *and* a mercenary. *A noble warrior.* That is who you are. Never forget it.

"Remember, I'm here with you. Your new friends are here with you. Your wife and family are with you if you let them. I think even Eric could be your ally, allowing you to be the best you while he is your complement. From today forward, you are not alone. You weren't made to walk alone. You never need to."

This is the moment I have been waiting for. I've never felt more confident that I can slay my dragon. The hairs standing on my arm now have nothing to do with the lightning. I feel an energy in my body that is transcendent. No one has ever spoken such words of belief in who I am and what I am destined to accomplish. I know that I am not alone. I can feel something deep like never before. Freedom. Peace. Confidence.

13

OFF THE MOUNTAINTOP

I really don't want the weekend to end. But it has to. Mark steps on a tree stump, whistles loudly, and asks everyone to gather around.

"This has been a great time together. The mentors here have all talked about what an amazing group we had this weekend. I think everyone here has taken very big steps to becoming a Thriver. We believe you all will continue on this journey and will have an exponential impact on this world. We soon will be sharing with each of you a gap analysis of what you need to do to become a Thriver. You now are aware that there is a gap, but the real work begins when you get down the mountain. Some of you are in the Goldminer's Quadrant, so we will give you access to ongoing coaching that will help you bring more meaning and purpose to your business. Others of you are in the Martyr's Quadrant, so you will receive training on how to better execute - how to sharpen your sword.

"I have a couple of final thoughts that I would like to leave you with. What we have taught you is how to thrive in today's world, which is about how to thrive in an economy built on Adam Smith's mindset of scarcity. When we navigate in such an economy, the competition that results is brutal, which is why you must learn how to fight. In this economy, the missionary mindset is not enough; you must also equally embrace the mercenary mindset. I intentionally used the word *mercenary* to wake you up to understanding what it takes to thrive.

Don't lose your heart as you learn to swing your sword. I am not the first to say that this life is a journey and not a destination, so give yourself grace as you fall down. Because no doubt, you will. I hope this weekend you learned that the important lesson of self-awareness and that you've determined to embrace how this life is designed to flow in a direction to shape your personal growth. This growth will be painful at times. I'm reminded of my favorite quote from the Baal Shem Tov, a Jewish mystical rabbi... *"Let me fall if I must fall; the one I am becoming will catch me."*

"Let me fall if I must fall; the one I am becoming will catch me." —Baal Shem Tov

---

The world is changing like no time in human history. We are experiencing a growth in consciousness accompanied by a rapid expansion of exponential technologies. Because of these factors, I believe an economy of abundance will replace our economy of scarcity. And this abundance is not just for the lucky few. I am not trying to be preachy at all, but even Jesus talked about much fruit and overflowing joy being produced from lives characterized by an abundance.

Mark paused for a moment and Maya jumped in. "I

heard the Dalai Lama say something similar just recently. He said '*I think there's every reason this 21st century will be much happier'.*"

"Exactly!" Mark said. "We are in the generation that this could be true for all of humanity. And that's what this is all about — adding true value to humanity. And where there is exponential value being created, there is abundance.

"It's not that capitalism is dead, but as our society continues to evolve through new ideas and exponential technologies, the invisible hand may be evolving into a better and more humane version of itself. This is not a shift to socialism, which would merely be a shift to another power structure. I believe in a world where what is best for you and what is best for humanity can coexist.

"The centralization of wealth and power in the hands of relative few will be changing because of technology that allows people and communities to decentralize. Smaller communities will be able to build their own economic systems and create their own rules. The centralized power structures and principalities of today may soon decay. I realize that I am introducing a very difficult concept with my closing remarks, but I am trying to whet your appetite for more. The economic systems of today are going to look very different in the near future. As stated by Buckminster Fuller, '*You never change things by fighting the existing reality. To change something, build a new model that makes the existing model obsolete.*'

"*You never change things by fighting the existing reality. To change something, build a new model that makes the existing model obsolete.*" —Buckminster Fuller

---

"So you're talking about basically changing the entire economic model?" Kyle asked.

"Exactly," Mark replied. "I bristle when I hear people complain that it can't be done. Change the model! Make it happen! Think! Get Creative! Just because it hasn't been done, doesn't mean it can't be done. We all have more power than we think to change the model. Including those without financial or institutional power. Think about it. Jesus, Gandhi, George Washington, Ben Franklin, Dr. King, Bill Gates and Steve Jobs proved that."

Even as Mark spoke, I could feel something shifting inside of me.

"The world is waiting for Thrivers who can lead the way toward this disruption, this evolved economy, this revolution for humanity. We are looking for those leaders who will wield the sword for good because of the longing in their hearts for a better world."

I looked around. Evan's eyes were locked on Mark. He seemed captivated by what he was talking about. I was curious what he was thinking.

"Please consider coming back for our Advanced Retreat, to learn more about the coming culmination of a social, economic, and technological revolution. We'll send you more details in the coming weeks. Until then, work hard to bridge your gap to become a Thriver."

In that moment, I know that I want to be part of the force that is changing the world for good. Something in this world needs to change, and he has sparked my curiosity. I have a deep feeling that I will be back to Six Peaks.

There are hugs all around as our team gathers in the parking lot for final goodbyes. It's amazing how much you can grow to care for people in such a short period of time. It reminds me that I truly enjoy people, and a part of the enjoyment comes from letting each other be our authentic selves. We all make certain we have contact info for each other and promise to check in exactly one month later. Alex steps up and says, "I will make sure this happens, people. Trust me."

"The barbarian has spoken!" Evan says.

Everyone, most of all Alex, laughs deep and loud.

I really don't want this to end. But in a way, something else is beginning.

~

THE LAST PERSON I speak with is Jack. I want the opportunity to simply tell him *thank you*. I extend my hand to shake his.

"Thank you, Jack. A part of me could stay up here on the mountain forever."

"Don't I know it. But the whole point is to go back down the mountain, return to the people and places we've committed to, and live out the example of a Thriver. I believe this about you, Chad. You are an overcomer. I cannot wait to hear how the days ahead unfold. Here's another little something to remind you of this place though."

Jack hands me a small leather-bound journal. The front cover is embossed with a simple marking...an infinity symbol.

"For the next thirty days, I want you to take time every day to write down at least three things you're grateful for. Some days you may have a lot more than three. Other days, you may only have three, but you've got to write at least three. Your dragon isn't dead, but it has been seriously wounded. And here's a surprise—it's really not about killing the dragon. In reality it's about taming the dragon. It will continue to scorch you at times with its fiery breath. Chad, now you've seen and can recognize the dragon, and you know how to fight it. Practicing mindfulness will be important. And this

119

daily practice of acknowledging what you are grateful for will be like swinging Excalibur in the fight. Deal?"

"Deal," I say. And with that, Jack gives me one last handshake, turns, and walks away.

"Hey, wait," I say. "Am I going to see you on the plane again?"

Jack smiles. "No, we'll be up here another day. But I'll think about you and our team when I look down at this valley from the cave. And well, you just never know when I'm going to show up again."

With that, I turn and walk to the Jeep. I sit down in the front seat and open the journal.

Chad aka "Warrior,"

Trust and embrace your name—your true self—and fight well for the people who love you. And there are many who do. You're a good man. A noble warrior.

Remember, each day write down three things you are grateful for, and every day practice your mindfulness.

Don't forget the mountain's lessons. And always know that I have your back.

Your friend,

Jack

DRIVING BACK DOWN THE MOUNTAIN, I can't help but think about Maggie. Historically, she is able to wield more of a mercenary mindset, and it is one of the things I love about our marriage. People always compliment the way we work together. I realize that I need her and, yes, she needs me. I feel a renewed passion to be a better man for my wife and children.

Suddenly, my phone blows up. I realize it is the first

time, except for the one text message exchange, that I've used my phone in three days. I pull over at a gas station, and without checking all my e-mails or text messages, I dial Maggie.

"Chad, is that you?" she says.

"Hi, Mags."

There's a pause.

"I wanted to call you to tell you how much I love you."

"I love you too, Chad. We didn't say goodbye very well, so we've still got some things to talk about when you get home. But I told you this was going to be good for you." I can almost see her smiling on the other end.

"So what is it? Why the difference in your voice?" she asks.

"I think I was reminded who I really am. And I can tell you this, Maggie. I'm going to love you and the kids better than ever. That's my first thing. And I'm not going to go down with Sensors Everywhere without a fight. I'm not going to go quietly into the night. I'm going to use wisdom and grace but also grit and courage."

Did I really just say that?

Then Maggie says the one phrase that has become our own little code for *everything's gonna be okay*.

"Go get 'em, Tiger!"

She knows that is my favorite line from one of the *Spider-Man* movies! With that call to battle, I feel like I could slay ten dragons. I smile and hang up after saying goodbye and then quickly scroll through my other messages.

There are several from Eric.

ERIC: Hey Chad, the VCs called me. They insisted that I meet with them. I told them you were out, but they said it couldn't wait. Hope that's cool with you.

ERIC: Chad, I just got back from a meeting with the

VCs. It was good, but I don't know. I'm not as sold as I was last week. Hope you're doing well.

ERIC: Hey man, I've been thinking about this deal. I'm here to support you. I trust you. You've got the vision for this. Whatever you decide, I'm in. I'm in your corner.

Then it hits me—Eric. What have I been thinking? It's as obvious as the Jeep I'm driving. My dragon has been lying to me the whole time about what Eric has been up to by meeting with InvestCorp. Eric is a mercenary through and through. It is the reason I hired him to begin with. As much as I've never embraced it, Eric has been the perfect complement to my missionary mindset from the beginning. But like Alex and that raft, I've never let go enough to allow him to fully help me. Micromanaging Eric and the team serves no one, not Sensors Everywhere, not Eric, and certainly not me. How have I missed that all these years?

I take a deep breath, inhaling as much of the pine in the air as I can. I instinctively focus on my breathing and can't help but smile as I do. For a moment, the world fades away. Then I look in the rearview mirror and see my face.

I'm not driving down the mountain a completely changed man, but I am going home more awake and aware. I am blessed with Maggie and the kids, a strong business partner in Eric, a devoted team of employees committed to Sensors Everywhere, and a new group of like-minded friends working toward that same goal of thriving and making this world a better place for us all. As Tolstoy said, "*What more can the heart of man desire?*"

I grab the steering wheel and have to pause. I notice that the Thriver's Signet on my finger is embedded with an infinity symbol, designed with three arrows indicating a never-ending flow.

That's what I feel after this weekend. There seems to be a flow of life that is good and is for me. Call it the infinite life, infinite love, or maybe it's what so many of us call God.

Too many unusual events happened this week that it would be crazy to describe it as merely coincidence. Yes, there is opposition or dragons, but something deep within my soul tells me that the good flow of life can be trusted. I need to learn to let go. From this moment on, I will wear the ring to remind me of this truth that I discovered on the mountain.

As I begin to pull out of the gas station, another text pops up on my screen. It's from another major VC group. They want to meet me on Monday. They say they've heard about me, and they're serious about working with me.

Well now, this could get interesting. Yes, I can do this. I am an overcomer. I am a noble warrior. Watch out, world!

I like this voice.

EPILOGUE

A *year later* . . .
    I drive back into Six Peaks in a Jeep, just like I had before. But things are different now. The cabins and trees and leaves feel familiar, but I have changed. A year has passed since the first retreat at Six Peaks. I check in and walk into the main meeting room to look around. The same round tables are scattered around with eager participants gathered at each one. I scan the room a bit closer and spot some familiar faces.

It wasn't the first time I'd seen them since the Entrepreneur's Retreat. After we'd all returned home, Jack had called each of us and invited us to be part of a mastermind group. He reminded us that "individually we are one drop but together we are an ocean." He told us that if we wanted to be truly experience transformation, we couldn't do it alone. And so we all agreed to meet once a week for a conference call. But that wasn't all. Since we'd all learned each other's strengths, each of us would call the others as we needed them. Well, almost all of us.

"Individually we are one drop. Together we are an ocean." —
Ryunosuke Satoro

AT THE TABLE next to me, Kyle is talking with a sharp-looking
young guy. Kyle looks more alive than ever. In the year since
the first retreat, we've become foxhole friends. The rafting
incident—and more importantly, what he took away from it
—has been his wake-up call. He's told me he is in the best
shape of his life, in every way. His business is better, his family
is vibrant, and he almost looks like an athlete. As Kyle talks
with the young entrepreneur sitting with him, I could guess
what they are talking about. One thing is certain—it has
something to do with swinging a sword.

At another table, I see Alex and Maya sitting together,
listening to the others in their group tell their stories—of life
and business and battles and shadows. Sitting on the table in
front of Alex is a small stack of books. I know what they are.
Copies of her new book. She'd sent me a signed manuscript a
few months earlier. She'd done it. Well actually, *they'd* done it.
Shortly after that first retreat, Alex brought Maya on as a
creative director for both her company and herself personally. Together, they'd penned a story for the ages. I don't think
Maya will be a starving artist ever again.

As for me? Well, I'm doing better than I ever imagined.
I'm learning to hold the sword and live from my heart at the
same time. And it shows. I've worked hard on my relationships with my wife and kids, and we are doing much better.
At the company, I've stepped back a bit. I'm still the corporate evangelist and chairman of the board, and I still have the
nickname "The Closer," but Eric is the CEO now, and he's
the best thing that ever happened to our company.

Oh, and remember InvestCorp? Well, not only did we end up doing a deal with them, but they've proven to be our new secret weapon…and some of my truest friends. At first, the InvestCorp team was intimidating but after the retreat, I realized their value and learned to embrace them as mercenaries *on my side!* Now, I can look back at that first meeting in their boardroom and realize that these guys never meant to diminish me — turns out they wanted the best for me and SensorSystems, they respected me even more once I listened to their advice and learned some mercenary skills for myself.

Looking around the room now, I know that everyone is here for the same reason I am. We all need to take our leadership and personal growth to the next level. We've learned one of the foundations of leadership—awareness—but now we need to go deeper.

But I'm forgetting someone. Evan, the hotshot tech entrepreneur. Well, Evan's story hasn't turned out exactly like any of us had hoped. After the retreat, Evan went back home and found himself right back in the same bad habits. He wasn't willing to pace himself and embrace the importance of culture and mitigating risk…and it cost him. Don't get me wrong—his company survived. But he crashed. Quite literally. His BMW i8 was found demolished somewhere in Nevada, and he was found wandering nearby. After that, he finally quit the company and walked away from it all. And for almost a year, none of us heard from him. Until the letter arrived. We each received a copy. I unfold mine and re-read it.

To: You Happy Few

This is Evan. I'm so sorry for the lack of contact. Things haven't been going exactly as planned. I lost heart with my work because it lost deeper meaning in my life, so it all imploded. I fell hard, but as Mark talked about, the person I am becoming caught me. I quit my company and traveled the world and focused on getting well. I think it worked. After that, I thought I could just walk away from it all . . . but I couldn't. I jumped back in.

I'm back in because of the hope I see in the decentralized economy and technology Mark talked about at the end of the retreat last year: the technology is called blockchain. Around the world, I've seen so many people living lives without abundance or even a simple identity. But now I know this can all change. My missionary passion has been reignited. I believe this is so important, but I need your help, You Happy Few. I'll tell you the rest of my story and why I call you the "Happy Few" at the Advanced Retreat. I'll be there. —Evan

Even as I finish reading the letter, I hear a familiar voice.

"Chad!"

I look up. It is Jack. He is walking in the back door of the room with Evan. The two of them make a beeline right for me. Kyle and Alex and Maya join us. We greet each other, and I can't help but notice the signet ring on Evan's finger. He notices mine, too.

"I know," he says. "For way too long, I wasn't living it. But things are different now. I was out of the good flow of life. But I've decided to get back up and jump back in."

And with that, the lights dim and Mark steps onto the platform.

"Welcome to EMERGE, our Advanced Retreat!" he says. "Congratulations . . . you made it through the first true test of leadership—awareness. Over the next few days, you'll learn how to apply more disciplines and values to your life and your business, and if you truly embrace them, they will forever change you."

I carefully read the words on the whiteboard.

The Six Peaks:

1. Story and innovation
2. Health and wellness

3.Awareness and authenticity

4.Leadership and culture

5.Operational excellence

6.Mentoring

Am I hallucinating, or does the first character in each of those Peaks spell "SHALOM"? As Mark begins to talk, I can see each person at our table listening with rapt attention. Evan is smiling from ear to ear. It is then that I realize we have only just begun our journeys together. That much is certain. I glance down at the ring on my finger . . . things are coming full circle now.

It feels good to be in the infinite flow. I can sense that I have aligned myself with something good that is in motion.

WHAT NEXT?

We hope you've enjoyed Thrivers and that you've learned something from Chad's journey that you can apply to your own story. We know that where you go from here is critical and we'd love to invite you to take the next step in your entrepreneur's journey.

You can dig deeper into the Thriver's Quadrant, explore the secrets of Six Peaks and discover much more than we've included in this book online at thrivers.com. We are continually adding new information, articles, podcasts and opportunities to join us for real-life Entrepreneur's Retreats.

Thank you for taking the time to read Thrivers. Now, will you join us in making a decision to go from scarcity to abundance and from business survival to making an exponential impact? See you online!

Visit us at www.thrivers.com

VANCE BROWN

Vance Brown is the CEO of the National Cybersecurity Center. He also is Chairman and Co-founder of Cherwell Software, recognized as one of the fastest growing companies in North America in 2014 and as the top software company in Colorado in 2015. Formerly, Vance was President and CEO of GoldMine® Software, one of the top 100 software companies in the United States at that time.

Vance was named EY Entrepreneur Of The Year™ 2014 Award Winner in technology and in 2017 was named one of the "100 most intriguing entrepreneurs" by Goldman Sachs.

Vance is a graduate of Wake Forest University and the University of North Carolina School of Law. Finishing on Law Review and Order of the Coif, Vance then mostly practiced law in the area of intellectual property.

Vance serves on the board for charitable organizations such as Parents Challenge, Care and Share and the Legacy Institute. He also is founder and chairman of a Colorado Springs non-profit technology accelerator called Exponential Impact. He is an Honorary Commander to the United States Air Force Academy.

JOHN BOLIN

JOHN BOLIN is an entrepreneur and storyteller passionate about encouraging others to use their talent to create opportunities to be remarkable and make an exponential impact.

As a speaker and consultant, he works with companies to help them clarify and amplify the stories of their customers. His upcoming podcast and video blog will feature entrepreneurs & creators who are crushing it doing what they love.

John is CEO of Bridgehouse.tv, a creative agency serving corporate clients and the entertainment industry. In addition to features, Bridgehouse works with authors, agents and companies to help them bring their content to life.

John is the author of 9 books including his debut novel The Eden Project, a thriller that combines action, adventure and nanotechnology.

John has shared the stage with Norman Schwarzkopf, Marcus Buckingham and John Maxwell and has presented keynotes for crowds from 500-10,000. John speaks regularly on the topics of maximizing life, story & creativity.

Made in the USA
San Bernardino, CA
20 September 2018